ELSEWHERE

BY THE SAME AUTHOR

ELSEWHERE

Collected Poems of
Nicholas Murray

THE MELOS PRESS

THE MELOS PRESS

First published in 2022 by
The Melos Press
38 Palewell Park
London SW14 8JG

Acknowledgements are due to the following periodicals in which many
of these poems were first published: *The Dark Horse, London Magazine,
Metre, New Boots and Pantisocracies, New Walk, New Welsh Review, Other
Poetry, Oxford Poetry, Planet, Poetry Durham, Poetry Salzburg Review,
Poetry Wales, The Rialto, Scintilla, The Spectator, The Tablet, Thumbscrew*
and *The Times Literary Supplement*.

'Blitz' was first published in *The Poet's View: Poems for Paintings in the
Walker Art Gallery, Liverpool* (1996) edited by Gladys Mary Coles.
'Walk' was the winner of the 2015 Basil Bunting Award.

ISBN 978-1-8381701-9-6

Typeset by CB editions, London
Printed in Great Britain by The Dorset Press, Dorchester DT1 1HD

For Sue

CONTENTS

GREEK LETTERS (2021)

THE NARRATORS

Landscapes

I dream of unreachable landscapes,
contours of plausible fiction
mapped by the mind's fertility.

Somewhere the purposeful beasts
leave rapid tracks in the snow;
a curious bird flies through the hot forest;

an undiscovered insect crawls,
unknown to the man in khaki shorts
who writes books in the winter.

One morning I shall rise with the sun
carrying the huge key to the garden,
turn the lock and look out

onto a wilderness of rhododendron,
stagnant lakes and broken summerhouses,
a fissured urn bursting with weed.

The Narrators

From hand to hand they pass the polished stick;
the fire crackles, sparks dance
above the shifting tray of logs.

Their god is linear; he has an end
and a beginning; is unamused by plotless anarchy.
The stick is smooth with continuities,

anonymous hands, forgotten tellers
tonguing remembered tales.
Invention is sudden, like a leap of sparks:
it comes, it goes, delays the stick

but does not hold it back.
It was a branch, sap-sticky once,
in leaf before its cutting down.

The Survivors

After the first inadequate fires
they discovered method,
kept coals alive and posted boys
to shout from plateaux at a sail.

There was talk of government
and the elders picked up their old ways,
affecting gravity and beards
as a reproach to folly.

The young were naturally flippant
constructing games in their own clearing;
recovering the procedures of sex
which flourished in auspicious weather.

Philosophers grew like gourds,
marvelling at the recurrence of order,
while moralists performed from rocks
anatomies of lust or greed.

After the first crops came science,
graphs sketched on the bald rock.
The talk came round to machines:
impatience of the post-pastoral.

The Transaction

Hand me the gold pen
with its sleek barrel;
I shall sign away
acres not mine.

And afterwards champagne
brought by a pale girl
whose tray clatters
in nervous hands.

We shall take lunch
in the tall room
which overlooks the river.
Beneath us barges rust

or swing at anchor;
a dog barks at the prow;
a bucket is emptied
into the swift stream.

And I settle
to a civility of forks
and white linen;
a crisp hors d'oeuvre.

A Plate of Spaghetti

These are the wide, incredulous eyes of Harpo Marx,
handed a plate which will soon be filled
with the tangled cordage of fresh spaghetti.

They speak of astonishment at such reversals
when the out-of-luck come into their own
and the least they can do is eat up.

The post-prandial concert is inevitable.
They are singing after supper their only song:
We have only our talent and our hunger to give you;

we are the century's displaced, the scuttling survivors
who seem to travel light but whose baggage
is weightier than any braced trunk deep in the hold.

The Suicide

The police broke in, astonished to discover
(though professionally attuned to wonder)
the council flat, its walls papered with poems
(Shakespeare's sonnets typed on scrap).

There was no bulb; their torches leered
at 'old December's bareness', Blu-Tacked
to a papered wall of red roses on a cream base.
'remembrance of things past' set out in caps

on the verso of a council tax demand (unpaid).
And in a chair the sonnet-bibber splayed,
a whisky bottle in his crotch, a dirty magazine,
the empty phial of pills, a scribbled note.

Open and shut case. No other sod involved.
Lonely and mad just like the others:
making worlds of wild coherence, run by laws
of madcap logic, ending, like any other, here.

Der Führer

Not wishing to see the ruined towns,
the gap-toothed terraces,
the cratered fields,
he ordered that the blinds be drawn
on the windows of his private train,
as if truth were inconvenient light
needing only a parchment shade;
or a framed view from which one steps,
swiftly, into another room.

History

The tall girl from Kildare,
I imagine you among horses and wide fields,
having taken the fence you faltered at,
marrying your man with the stubbled chin
and the slow, gentle smile.
On our bar stools, just the two of us,
like an emblem of innocence and experience,
we rehearsed your story: dismantled dreams
when his car left the country road
and your heart, untenanted, searching,
came to ask itself if happiness was the four walls
of a good man's house who would not survive you.

On a lift into town, he stopped at a barley field,
waded out like a fisherman in shallow seas,
to stare at the blank horizon as if a message
were posted for his attention,
and came back to the Land Rover, saying nothing.

Our game of tennis at dusk, the lost ball we foraged for
in the long grass where our hands brushed lightly
and you turned away, saying nothing.

Do you rule now a flagged kitchen
in a big house among fields,
or do you trim the plant of a single life
with expert fingers, sheathed in a green glove?

Osteopath

Look at this stately dance
as she takes my arm and twists it round
first this way, then that,
from this and then that angle;
spinning me round with the clodhopping grace
of folk dance on a museum forecourt.
Every bit of me turned and twisted
to loosen the inflamed cordage of pain.
Afterwards, we inspect the red anatomical man,
sitting side by side, like two children
on a companionable swing.

Pleasure

First pleasure comes, and then its payment, pain.
In cold, grey light the lovers deftly leave,

close doors and quickly scatter down the stairs
of flats whose tenants neither know nor care.

A tower of cartons in a city mews;
a magnum placed against a vacant door.

They turn again: was it a trick of light?
There is no argument in natural air.

No way to be deceived, to scotch the facts:
first pleasure comes, and then its payment, pain.

First Day Of Summer

All day the sun had struggled with this paste
of lumpy cloud, occluded light and hampered heat,
until, late afternoon, the curtain rolled away
and sunlight splashed the gravel yard
where two club-chairs of royal blue were set,
their canvas warming in the sudden rays.
A fat and dizzy bee clambered among weeds;
sheep gathered to the nettles at the field's corner;
somewhere beyond trees a beast bellowed;
and cooing pigeons, like a late band, set up in the still ash.

Fourfuls

1
Were I a speaker of Welsh
I should let the language speak
through difficult rhymes of *englyn*,
forcing its way to the front, like an impatient child.

2

The flattened form of a buck-rabbit
made slow by old age
slithers under my gate
like the last, disappearing page.

3

I have reached middle age.
A gate between two fields:
one crossed in a careless loop and dawdle,
the next with eyes trained on that well-shaped oak.

4

Cold Northerners, the olive tree completes us.
Its flash of silver-green, its plaited trunk,
ravaged in Gaza by the 'dozer's teeth:
the poor, as ever, bearing the brunt.

5

The dividends of Empire, overstated somewhat,
include Britannia's gift to Corfu
of the small bitter fruit from China,
its tangy thick liqueur: the kumquat.

Cyclists

They are out in all colours on Offa's Dyke.
Black Lycra legs; spiked gloves;
crash helmets; jockeys of the bike
that lightly bounces over rut and twig.

They are sealed within themselves,
intent, armoured in bright rig,
chasing pleasure with the grimness it deserves.
No time for me, no time at all:

the casual wanderer in normal shoes
pausing to pluck a wand of bracken
to scout the flies; stopping for views
of sleeping hills under sheets of mist.

A rabbit plumply settles on the track,
its tardily suspicious eye not yet on me
until I tread on fallen twigs that crack
a message of alarm to send it loping off.

Well-being spills with sunlight from a cloud
that opens like a clam to show a purer blue,
glinting through leaves, the sprinting crowd
of cyclists, fifty yards ahead, a bright flash.

Politics

Self-exiled, stowed below decks.
No sound but the thrum of engine gear,
the sporadic chorus of grey gulls,
and somewhere the tap-tap of a rust hammer
preparatory to paint.

What might tomorrow bring?
The thin line of a waterfront,
its daddy-long-legged cranes,
a rapid launch slicing towards us
with a cargo of loud hailers and braid?

Or will we float forever
on this soup-dark sea,
with no impulse to shout
or frame the right words
or the words thought right, once?

1946

This corner of a magazine
flutters from a bought book
where it has lodged, peacefully,
for fifty years.
Radio Times? Something that ends
in *'es'*, ripped off to mark a place
in a copy of Walton's *Lives*.

That was after the War,
a drab and rationed time
of powdered milk
and long macs,
bonfires by the black sleepers
upended to fence the allotment,
a few, blunt-nosed cars.

Or was it like that?
No way to know,
but this morning
you left, your hand warm,
the mist drying off,
love freshly shooting
like pages hot from the press.

Stone

At certain moments I felt that the entire world was turning into stone.
– Italo Calvino, *Six Memos for the Next Millennium*

Such that a tear taking its course on a cheek
might find its bead frozen for ever,
trapped in the glass-museum of grief.

And what should have been a passage out
through the arms of the harbour wall
to the far continent named on the ticket stub

becomes a grounding here – as vandals
and small boys clamber up to chip
at that increasingly ludicrous boss.

Greek Mythology

Generally overlooked, in spite of their position
at the start of things, in the Theogony section,
are the offspring of Ge and philoprogenitive Ouranos.
I'm talking Briareus, Gyes, and Cottos,
each boasting fifty heads and a hundred hands
and, I imagine, by Pater's example, a stock of glands.
Then their young siblings known as the Cyclopes
viz. Arges, Brontes, and Steropes
who were tied up and tossed into Tartaros gloom
and then, as if they weren't already out of room,
came the Titans: Oceanos, Hyperion, Iapetos, Coios,
not to mention young Cronos and, finally, Creios.
As is usual in these narratives of the ancient past
the girls were named and considered last:
Tethys, Themis, Mnemosyne, Rhea,

Phoebe, Dione, and (one more) Theia.
That Ouranos, on this evidence, was a champion breeder,
would I think be the view of any dispassionate reader.

Laurel

How Daphne might have felt
as she ran from the breathy Apollo
(before her skin was bark, her feet roots,
her arms boughs in wild semaphore,
her fingernails the bitter leaves
destined for a victor's crown)
I felt in that nightmare of pursuit
one is always destined to wake from.

The Libation-Bearers

Even armed with my synopsis,
and fresh from a new translation
I accept that this is risk
of a high order: *Aeschylus in Greek!*

Self-taught, self-stalled in rudiments,
transliterator merely, who can write:
the Persians are pursuing the Greeks,
and catch 'tomb', 'father', 'messenger'   .

I sit, attentively, to watch
the clever students do their stuff,
hauling those words back to life,
walking a little stiffly on the stage.

And then, the real reward:
the curtain parts and Clytemnestra
bursts, in a red dress, from downstage.
Big hair, big voice, a passionate London Greek.

Sycophant

The word's from those whose fingers slyly pointed out
the lifters of fresh figs from private orchards.

At the rack-and-pinion railway's foot
this skinny ancient works the end-of-summer crowd,
his little cart piled high with figs.
Kalavryta's hot Sunday crush
hears: *Sika freska! Sika freska!*

Our fingers point to where the fresh figs are.

Ithaca

A harbour so perfect in its enclosing arms
we arrogant humans say: is it natural?
and think of Ulysses with his salt-caked skin
enjoying the long aftermath of war.
Travelling (as Cavafy says in his wise poem)
being much the better part of arriving:
like a book whose last chapter we evade,
recalling a need to put a light to the gas ring
or accomplish any of a dozen light tasks
that might include placing a log on the dying stove.
After that, the tucking of a bookmark in the page
and tapping the closed book on one's knee,

admiring the jacket design which tempted us
in a shop of piled volumes, all deliciously unread.

Greek Islands

Samothrace
Too early in April to enter the blue sea
we went to the ruins whose keeper kept chickens
and a key to the stockade of fallen marble
that ran to the shore through carpets of flowers.
From here the winged Victory
flutters its wings in a plaster cast
(one more room to be unlocked).

Aegina
The fury of the fish restaurant
and the greed of a fatman
licking his lips
and calling out for another carafe
of chilled retsina,
another plate of battered squid.

Nissyros
The blue lupins on the mountain road
are all that I would wish to note.

Hydra
I would have disembarked
but the young woman in black
with a mobile phone
and a cellophaned sandwich
put the idea in my head
of moving on to the next port.

14

Samos
A meal at the harbour's edge,
mist coming in off the sea;
mist on the chilled bottle
of dry, Samian wine.

Crete
The wild flowers of Rethymnon
near battlements built against the Turk.

Ithaca
A white beach where I lay in the sand
like someone resting after a long voyage;
like someone tired by a year of work
still running in my head like an angry crowd.

Kos
Arriving at dawn, the sun not yet up,
and a slumped figure at a cafe table
watched by a glass, half-full,
or half-empty, depending on the point of view
of a somnolent, staggering, wasp.

Tinos
A curtain twitched; a bony finger hooked us in
to a crone's cottage, scattered with straw;
a shy husband bringing in a basket
that hangs now from our pitted beam.

Delos
And the water in between,
someone shouting: *'Delfini!' 'Delfini!'*
Smooth, peaceable things we shall see on shore
carved on white stone.

Mykonos

The pink pelican has stepped out of a postcard
for a stroll along the front,
an early evening photo-shoot,
hamming it up, lifting its big beak
like a supermodel flaunting herself
in a public park amid lights and white screens.

Himself a Poet

Oh yes, we all know the truthfulness of blurbs:
like the grocer's insistence that his gnarled loaf
with its scatter of grains, signalling wholesomeness,
was not drawn, craftily, from the freezer at dawn.

Three Versions of Liverpool

1

The empty squares in summer;
a crumbling elegance of sandstone
where a sash window opens

to reveal a girl combing her hair,
long, red, Rapunzel hair,
Scouse-vowelled 'hur'.

And in the streets no-one
but bus-stop loiterers,
two drunks, a priest

16

with a determined stride
like a gamekeeper
hunting poachers.

2

A cluttered history of ships
and Irish migrants,
dark, wheedling priests

who ruffled hair to ask:
'Will he become a priest?'
I see their pale skulls shine

in living rooms where kin
once crowded with their songs,
doing the hokey-cokey:

thin uncles, sharp as knives,
with heads like street-maps,
the city in their veins.

3

A foreign coaster racing out
between the plying ferries
gives a deckhand's wave.

A cloud of gulls descends
where crusts are thrown,
wheeling on tides of air.

So little cargo now:
the high-decked liners,
tall and white, removed.

Their linen and their knives
sold off at auction
at a knock-down price.

North

Were it not for the airbag of warm humour,
bibulous laughter, the chink and shout
of a good time, my bones would crack.

In my speech there is studded the flat 'a'
which I shall never prise off; nor the memory
of men with bicycles staring out to sea;

the ham and salad teas; the Christmas cake
brought out, put back, unscathed until New Year,
its snowmen, sleighmen, clamped in ice.

'Down to earth' the boast at this smoky do.
But I dream of the giddiness of flight,
the brilliance of cold air, and silence.

Obol

Standing out in all weathers,
gloves stuffed in an epaulette,
silver buttons gleaming on the grey coat,
a peaked cap for doffing.
Obsequious as the job demanded,
but with higher ambitions.

His first job – holding the bridles
of Liverpool tram horses.
He would later rise to a firm's car
which took him daily to the warehouse
on the Dock Road to drink in deference
of a kind he had meted out
at the glass doors of the Bon Marché.

The grandfather I never knew,
who, falling dead in church,
my father helped to carry back
and up the twisting stairs, recording
later in his diary, how a silver coin
rolled from the dead man's trousers to the floor.

The Room

That room which seemed so large
swells with each fictive retrospect.

We re-arrange our courting places
to the correct taxonomies.

Even that oval table dragged
to meet a skylight which allowed

twilight perspective of slate roofs,
the sluggish river at low tide,

seems like some vast boardroom conceit –
not bleached and spotted with old ink.

But truly there's no need to amplify,
for what's imagined can't compete

with that dark stairwell
and the heavy door beneath

which closed too often
on too many narrow nights.

Your Photograph

Look where it stands,
skew-whiff upon a pile of books
in its nerveless cardboard frame.
Behind you a perfect Sicilian sky,
wild poppies and the hint of ruins.

An adequate paradigm of love:
half like an icon, half profane.
Distracted wholly by its glare
no work is done today
and resolution trickles off like sand.

Unopened books conspire like crowds
in charcoal suits and proper hats
who shame the pavement loafer
with his belt of string.
Gilt spines declare: *get on, get on.*

Blitzkrieg

Grainger Smith, *The Enemy Raid*, Walker Art Gallery, Liverpool

Like some outrageous sunset seen from Waterloo,
destruction flowers, filling the sky with flame.
Fires on the Dock Road, two sisters hurrying home
from Blackpool where a brother in the RAF (who never flew)
was left quite safe; but now, like snapping sparks,
their fears rise up again and join with others' on the street:
the ripped-out house front that a soldier home on leave
suddenly gasps at; unnatural light flooding the parks;
young girls (excited or afraid) beneath a kitchen table
in a street in Seaforth, all its windows patched with black.

These are the legends we absorbed: they now come back
to children of the Welfare State who are not able
to imagine how a world of wooden huts dispensing orange juice,
cod liver oil, and ration-books now items in a junk-shop sale
grew out of this: dark raids, the siren's sudden wail,
a night of restless fear groping towards dawn's truce.
The wardrobe in my parents' room, whose stippled door
of deep-embedded Blitztime glass was like a tale
our childish fingers traced in halting Braille,
was all we had to touch of that imagined War.

Family Life

We all know what Larkin
(lugubrious, lustful librarian)
had to say about one's folks.

but it's possible to break free:
or, failing that, to say no, once,
before one croaks.

To Live in Wales

Is to be conscious that the clock
ticking in a tall walnut case
will shortly sound, after muffled whirrs,
the noise of midnight: time to go.

Rugs lie on the slate floor;
on the massive table (thrown out
by a Carmarthen butcher and retrieved
one gleeful auction afternoon).

A handmade bowl of succulent beans
cools; bottles wander to refill
the pottery goblets; and a knife
slices another wall of cheese.

Eight faces in the candlelight
chatter and make laughter
in a pair of cottages
annexed into one

whose slate roof, patterned with moss,
holds cooing pigeons, or, as now,
the monitory owl whose call
is drowned by vivid talk.

In the lane, like dark cattle,
the expensive cars cluster,
hardly visible in the dark
until a bright light bursts from the door.

What Thought Did

'Went behind a muck-cart,' my father said,
'and thought it was a wedding.'
A thought which returned to me,
as it were from the dead,
when I stalled behind the yellow cart
where men hung like languid postilions,
on the hottest day of June,
their thick boots on the metal rung,
wasps homing in on the stinking hatch.

Honfleur

for Sue

In Satie's mad museum
on Saint Sylvester's Eve
we wander through the rooms,
our minds elsewhere,
as a white piano
plays itself, endlessly.

It is a kind of carnival
at the year's end.
Next day we move on
to sleepy Rouen
where we claim
our round red table

amongst smiling gourmands
who do not know our secret:
the one we place between ourselves
like a napkin in its ring.

How does one do it, such a toast?

How honour the years?

GET REAL!

On 12th May 2010, six days after the British general election had result-
ed in no party having an overall majority, David Cameron and Nick
Clegg, leaders respectively of the Conservative and Liberal Democrat
parties, agreed to form a coalition Government. The coalition immedi-
ately proposed a massive programme of cuts in government spending,
unforeseen in its extent in either of the two parties' manifestos. To their
critics this was motivated more by an ideological desire to roll back the
frontiers of the state than by fiscal prudence. On 9th December 2010
the coalition Government, following proposals from Lord Browne, chief
executive of BP at the time of the 2010 Gulf of Mexico oil spill, agreed
to allow student tuition fees to be increased to £9000 a year, in spite of
Liberal Democrat election candidates having signed public pledges never
to agree to the existing cap on fees being removed. As a result, large and
sometimes violent student protests erupted in central London towards
the end of 2010.

1

The politics of 'coalition,' bite
and shop-soiled dogma of the Right
once more is back;
but, with a newer twist, it claims
to be absolved from party games,
debating points and calling names
'on track '

to make the 'undeserving poor',
unlike the rich, pay even more
as a proportion
of what they work for; learn austerity
from those who engineered 'prosperity'
and now prefer the masochist's severity,
and caution,

who once threw prudence liberally aside
in one long, mad, careering slide
of spending,
that it seems we can afford no longer
until the public purse is stronger;
and every overpaid doom-monger,
garments rending,

from comfy offices above the City,
with unconvincing tones of pity,
says 'Cut'
(except their lunches which are needed,
for, in those growing beds, are seeded
solutions, that if left unweeded,
would be *kaput*).

2

In January cold an east wind slices
the bleak estates with rising prices
for heating gas
and other costs of meagre living
where pensioners are daily giving
their household budgets careful sieving
that the crass

expenses-proofed glib politician
in his extraordinary rendition
calls 'sense'
and digs up putrid metaphors
from household budgets in the Wars
when cleaning-women knelt on floors
for pence.

They have the gall, these men in suits,
whose family cash is stowed in Coutts,
to lecture
the ones who haven't much, or less,
on how to exit from this mess,
that idiot bankers nonetheless
conjecture

requires more cash to be expended
on bonuses; who once extended
bad loans
to folk who couldn't pay, then foundered,
and from their skulls no echo sounded
of that much-mentioned 'sense' propounded
by drones

inside the hive of Con-Lib 'thinking'
and, while our finances are sinking,
they bawl
for more, like children at a birthday bash,
for whom the prospect of a crash
is something parents' brains must mash
or not at all.

3

Now students march and shout and chant
derisive mockery of Lib-Dem cant:
that vote,
where, having pledged themselves, they junked
their promise solemnly intoned, and funked
when through the lobbies each one slunk,
to emote

next day on breakfast radio shows
how hard it was to join the Noes:
my arse!
Their words that minds had never matched
hardly disturbed a conscience patched
with slimy get-outs, or they hatched
the farce

of choosing to abstain, not even able to say Yes,
left it to others to sort out the mess:
the shits!
(How anger makes our register decline
and decorous terms slip out of mind
and language quickly ceases to refine
our wits.)

The campus greens are now a smoking field
where pillage makes the conquered yield
a waste;
where all that grows is business prattle,
its empty, fatuous, unhelpful rattle,
and shifty dons concede the battle,
two-faced.

4

They would accomplish in a single year,
extreme contraction of the public sphere,
chop down
the wide-girthed oaks that centuries nurtured,
and in a jargon weaselly and turgid,
in which all promises are perjured,
blame Brown.

The richest nations forage for a coin,
and kick the poorest in the groin.
Hard luck:
the pension fund's now closed its door,
so don't place bids like Oliver for more;
spread out your cardboard on the floor;
we've no truck

with welfare scroungers, lazy unemployed,
the feckless who display the gaping void
of pockets
empty of sums we'd merely throw at waiters:
ugly, resentful, carping haters
of our Success – for whom the *Guardian* caters –
the sockets

of their eyes in envious hatred glowering,
who only think of petty, lowering
resentment
of those who make it by their wits alone
(don't mention the convenient loan,
or something Daddy promised on the phone).
Investment

in the future not the past's our motto.
While the proles spend cash on Lotto,
we secure
the sort of funds that make the Future bright
and watch, in grimmest times, the leaping light
of profit shining through recession's night,
its lure,

is like the star a hopeful boatman sees,
promise of dividend and copious fees
for us,
which 'trickles down' – don't they know this?
We are the true philanthropists
who think of Good alone and seldom miss
the bus.

For we are there to save the nation,
from its long slide to a stagnation,
that hurts
our pockets, too, your pain's our own;
our hearts are not made out of stone;
but we prefer to act, not moan:
stuffed shirts

of politicians spill their words like seeds,
on stony ground where nothing breeds,
the fools!
We know what works, what thrives, what ticks;
we're in the Real World and we know the tricks,
like the hungry dog that sees the bone and licks
and drools.

5

But there's no gratitude for Cameron-Clegg
who merely want to take a peg
that's square
and fit it to a hole that's round; they're sent
to recreate a nation that has spent
too little at the sales, like penitents in Lent.
Fair's fair:

We have to change; we can't go on, for sure,
Old Britain needs to take the cure,
renew its pelf.
We need to spend, and when that's done spend more,
produce, consume and then consume some more,
the old were thrifty but (you noticed?) *poor!*
The self

is where it's at today, the iPod generation knows
just where the rosy light of new dawn glows:
inside.
Society, the Iron Lady said, is just illusion,
a socialistic, muddle-headed, dark confusion,
and everyone can see the stark conclusion:
it died.

For Royal Mail or doctors without wait,
just quote your Visa card, don't ask the state.
For starters:
if the poor, who don't like work,
can get the same as I – and those who shirk
can match my salary and perk,
We're martyrs

in the cause of justice and of equal shares.
No way! That thinking's out of date as flares
or spats.
It's true the young have valueless degrees,
big debts, small hopes, no jobs, a freeze
on buying homes, bankrupt from fees
But that's

not my look-out; it's life, the shape of things;
it's what a look at hard facts brings:
you see?
There is no option but to grin and bear it
and what makes every politician dare it?
Give Brits a hair-shirt, they'll always wear it.
To infinity!

ACAPULCO

Icon

These angular, sad men
in pointed beards
and rivuleted cheeks

take down their Christ
and fondle him
like tender lovers.

Their pained eyes
ingest his agony,
their pinched hands,

gothic-arched,
seek pardon
for this imposition,

this surrogate hurt
that should have cut
their flesh not his.

Desire

Quick sprint of flame
through brittle straw . . .

Wind's impatience
with a loose tin roof . . .

Raptor's appetite,
sated on the wing . . .

Cry and carol
of daybreak's stir . . .

Like nothing, like nothing,
but itself.

Antaeus

The ground my strength,
my power common dirt;

simian, I crouch in dust,
ten fingers on the clay.

I'm poised to spring,
a coiled beast.

From your bright eyes,
comes mocking confidence

that one swift blow
could crush my power.

Tossed like a ball
from one to one,

held high and thrown
into the impotence of air,

you'd laugh to see
my energy dissolve.

I'll take all comers
where I stand or fall.

What do you wait for?
Look where my foot

drums on the ground,
beats out defiance.

Look, where a dust-cloud
dances in the sun.

Elsewhere

[Vilhelm Hammershøi, *Bedroom*, 1890]

How you anticipate
our love of the minimal:
this woman in her 1900s
black gown like a hand-bell
against the window-pane;
her back to us, held
in a garden of bare trees.

Your silence grows in us,
expands like rising dough,
until we reach the street
and find ourselves, altered,
in an exalted elsewhere.

Archaeologist

Hairless, his skull glistens; his lips are talking to themselves.
Rattling to Holborn on the Central Line, his triumph waits:
a paper on the hitherto unknown Swan People, allies of Boudicca,
whose trade was fire and symbol the cool, white swan.

They torched Londinium, their eyes ablaze, fire meeting fire,
watching the detumescent towers, the flame-licked doors,
gloating on destruction's bacchanale, its quick despatch
of villas, temples, workshops, houses, bright mosaic squares.

Unknown until, one afternoon at Cripplegate, his brush
uncovered fused medallions of the swan, like lovers tangled up
in overheated limbs: his mind shot forward as a line of flame,
connecting A and B; with two and two computing five.

Island Swimmer

She is too quick for me:
only a ripple as arms
slice through the calmed,
cooled sea, late afternoon.

Her deft, aquatic grace
reminds us of our clumsy,
walrus-like advance
towards the shore.

Her ancient skin
like supple leather
glistens in last light;
effortless, she emulates

the action of the eel,
that wriggles in the depths
beneath a white caique
which rocks beside the quay.

Emei Shan

Coughs and clattered sticks;
short laughter; puffs of breath

scribbled on dawn air;
a tense and waiting silence.

We have come for this:
a spreading stain

of tentative pink light,
deepening fire-red

as the sphere's bright rim
breaks the still surface

of a tranquil lake:
unruffled white.

We gather to our shelf
of jutting rock, chattering,

and then the gasp,
the shout of seeing.

The ritual done,
we quickly scatter

to the noise of breakfast:
pork noodle bowls,

rattle of chopsticks,
scald of green tea.

In each of us a quiver
of melting gold.

Culture Capital (2008)

1

On my boyhood beach
the rusting torsos
are hatted, by local wits,
in carrier-bags.

Gormley's men
sink in the sand,
their eyes fixed
on the thin strip of Wirral.

Another joke:
rubbery seaweed
fixed in place,
a sandy cache-sexe.

2

That's it, you see,
the famous 'Scouse humour'
that can wear thin
if you don't see the joke

like Anthony Walker
stabbed to death
in a park where hate
came to unzip itself.

3

Bulldozers, hard-hats,
high-viz. tabards:
the mulch from which springs
another shopping mall,

another sheet of glass
gingerly put in place
by someone high in a crane,
wondering how to pee

in the long stretch
before lunch,
his girders put down
like sticks of Kit-Kat.

4

A table of filled bumpers;
the Lord Mayor's chain
sagging on a fat belly
full of itself.

Regeneration's the tag
for culture's rôle,
putting a good gloss
on the usual business.

Money sings
like the imported tenor
who carols the triumph
of 'confidence'

and the canvasses
swung from a truck
in their wadding of
bubble-wrap

clinch the deal
with a wink
and a loud laugh
from the far end of the hall.

5

And always the gulls,
crying and swooping
for the inevitable
tossed titbit.

East

Did it come on the wind,
through the thickness of ancient forest,
at her grandmother's house by the lake:

the announcement of Spring,
the different taste of air,
and the chant of renewal?

Did she read, in the rustle of leaves,
or the cry of rooks in a high elm,
the first drafts of truth?

Ice: The Movie

I left her at the frozen port,
old tyres chafing the pier,
a ladder leading nowhere,
and the broken ice-sheets
overlapped, like mail
that's tumbled from a sack.

Her camera shouldered,
she set off in search of sunset
by the gelid sea,

her backpack dusted
with a flour of snow,
red gloves against the white.

She had been gone an hour
when winter light thinned out
and we grew anxious
in the little bar whose tubes
sent glittering shafts
across the hard-packed snow.

We looked at watch-dials,
listened to the radio,
consulted tipsy experts
in the bar's dark cul-de-sac:
weather-wise fishermen
and wordy bores.

Our resolution came,
high stools scraped back;
cold feet were stamped;
some went for torches,
tackle and ropes were fished
from locked and frozen sheds.

But she upstaged us
in the final scene.
Whirled round with grains,
exultant, cold, high-coloured,
she flung the door back
with a whooping laugh.

Our swagger detumesced;
tackle was angrily let go
as little pools of melted ice
patterned the planked floor;
nervously, a bearded giant
lifted and left her on the highest stool.

Sea Wind

Translated from Stéphane Mallarmé's *Brise Marine*

If books no longer work and flesh gives no respite
then join the sweeping gulls, drunk with delight,
whirling in new skies across strange seas.
Stop gazing on dead flowerbeds; don't freeze
in the unwritten page's chill, white, lamplit glare;
no duty's call from your young wife can keep you there.
You're off! Down to the harbour to the waiting steamer,
an eager, ambitious, Utopian dreamer.

Too much regret and tearful weeping
leaves the would-be rover sleeping.
Don't yield to fear that portside rigging
will soon vibrate in storm-wind's jigging,
and don't be tricked so that your dream
of luscious islands dulls its visionary gleam.
Don't weaken: hold fast to the sailors' shanties calling
and spring aboard while liberating night is falling!

Acapulco

for Elizabeth Neylan

Around the bay, with the brightness of beach-huts,
the tower blocks gather to the contemplation of blue;

the white table and chair are waiting for the man
in a garish shirt and the knobbliest of knees

whose serious aim is pleasure and the sting of sun
as the heat of the day is turned up.

But the question remains: will that pelican,
in its flat-footed fashion, get there first,

establish a bridgehead and order drinks,
usurping the seat of the languid tourist

who – just at that moment – is stepping from the bus,
his viewfinder getting in the way of the view.

Riddle

It is not here
or there
as objects are;

it has no smell,
no taste, no touch,
no sight, no sound

yet works
through these,
subduing all

to an imperative,
an iron law
we can't resist;

no life's untouched
by it; no heart
at all assuaged.

Gloss

All other things to their destruction draw,
    Only our love hath no decay
– John Donne, *The Anniversary*

Let Time attempt this granite rock
and wildest weather, wind and rain,
struggle to break its mass apart.

Or see it as brass foundry lock
that clamps a heavy iron chain
to bind the lightness of the heart.

ΤΟ ΓΙΑΣΕΜΙ

Είτε βραδιάζει
είτε φέγγει
μένει λευκὸ
τὸ γιασεμί
– George Seferis

The Jasmine

Eternal beauty
of the jasmine flower
that gleams at dusk
or at the day's first hour.

Orpheus

Orphée en tournant la tête
Perdit sa femme et ses chants.
Les hommes devinrent bêtes
Et les animaux méchants
– Lines of Jean Cocteau painted on his mural at a Salle des Mariages,
Hôtel de Ville, Menton

That we might imitate the beast was Cocteau's thought
for those who came to seek the blessing of the State
on bourgeois marriage in the bright Spring sun
that blazed along the morning's Côte d'Azur.
The beast in man's a common theme:
we are not always nice, but animals are slandered
when compared to butchers in the rigout of the State,
who kill without the need to eat or procreate.
Orpheus (who broke the rules and squandered
what he had, the love of sweet Eurydice, her dream
likewise dissolved) lost something more:
his gift of song, and everything he'd won
in singing contests in the Attic sun; too late
he found that in the trade of love grief's also bought.

Topping Out

'Life often looks like those palazzos on the Grand Canal where the
builder begins with splendidly ornamented, diamond-shaped stone
features but quickly finishes off the upper storeys in dried mud.'
– Paul Morand, *Venices*

How it takes time to find
the taste for one's rough self.

Slowly, I learn to prize
what once was crowded out:

a simple lodging in the roof
where birds fly past;

four walls, unpainted
to enclose a thought;

bare boards, a stage
where all's enacted

in the mind's quick theatre,
where no props distract;

a jar of roadside flowers
constructs its case

without the chisel's work,
or grand, pentelic boast.

Courage

for Peter Tatchell

Today is the day
to clean the streets
of the gay-proud.

The shavenskulls slip
like loosed dogs
into the chanting crowd

to scatter their mayhem
under the benevolent eye
of the 'security forces'

whose black boots
firmly cleave to
the frozen ground.

It is the mania of hatred:
each lashing out
at what he fears

like a man whose wild hands
fight off a swarm
of angry bees.

Food

On Midway Atoll they spread out the infant albatross:
its stomach slit to show the bellyful of plastic trash
that parents plucked from the polluted sea as food.

Spent lighters, bottle caps, blue, red and green;
detritus of the waves which made itself appear
as useful sustenance that beaks should clip

into the waiting mouths of hungry infant birds
spread wide to snatch at buoyant scraps,
like those we toss to pigeons in the square.

Owl

That cold, accusing look!
How it flops through the glass doors,
that I have opened wide,
granting it release from kindling smoke.

Something in that eye suggests
that I had brooded long on this offence
while in the chimney's dark it slept,
a sleep that latent malice would disturb.

Something in that eye suggests
that my intentions were not pure;
that when I put the match to twigs
I laughingly desired its pain.

The head that swivels round, the eye,
focus to condemn more fixedly
the vile tormentor, who, far too late,
let out the scalded, hopping thing.

That is the eye of judgement
that can't forget the cold malignity
I meant, the joy I took in anguish,
the smell of feathers lightly singed.

It is the unforgiving eye of dreams
that will not shut; it haunts my sleep;
the weight of misdemeanours stacked
like stones against a mason's wall.

The eye that pierces, finds all fault,
probes deep into the heart and sees
the store of things guilt slyly stores
foolishly thinking it can hide.

That eye turns back as out the door
it skips and jumps, regaining flight
just on the other side, feeling the comfort
of the sodden, cold, assuaging field.

Butterfly

For as long as it takes
(which is no time at all)
the red admiral settles
on its landing-strip of leaf.

Catch it if you can,
before the bright page closes
and all is green again,
only the thought remaining:

like a tempting phrase
that formed itself quickly
as the lights changed
from amber to green.

Wild Swimming

'As they call it now':
the covert wriggle into trunks,
a wobble on the bloom-blue stones,
then the icy contact, stage shivers,
and the seal-swift plunge
into the blinding baptism
of sea closing above one's head.

Afterwards, dried off,
we potter round the shack-shops
of late summer Borth:
the kitsch collectables
(a stand of meerkat, soldiers, kings),
smutty slogans on a giant mug,
the Brylcreem-goo of white ice cream.

A slick of wet hair,
still plastered to your cheek.

Autumn

The dying flowers at summer's end;
abundant fruit beneath the tree.

Wasps with their sluggish appetite
boring short tunnels in the flank of plums.

Our feet trudge paper shoals of leaf,
flail-cutters slash the raddled hedge.

And in the valley antique sun
gilds the rough stubble with its light.

The shortened days and cooling nights
are heralded by scented chimney-smoke.

We live with such repeats, the punchline
works though we can mouth it in advance.

Radnor

The pairs of sunning lambs,
spaced out around the field,
intuitive, quick in their grasp of comfort,
take their ancestral ease;

I'd like to emulate this trick,
to get the proper hang of it.
to laze the light-long day,
as if the drifts of snow and ice

were a forgotten episode,
and winter's cold,
its niggard way with light,
a blip between two suns.

Spring Equinox, 2011

The Song Of You

You are the seed; you are the flower.
You are the second; you are the hour.

You are the atom; you are the world;
You are the bud that the sun unfurled.

You are the dream; you are the real
You are the concept; you are the feel.

You are the whisper; you are the shout
You are the skirmish; you are the rout.

You are the hamlet; you are the town
You are the up and you are the down.

You are the drizzle; you are the storm
You are the rarity; you are the norm.

You are the creature deep in the night;
You are the glory and triumph of light.

You are the end and you are the start;
You are the furnace that flames in my heart.

Tell Me the Story

Tell me the story; how did it start?
How did you shatter the lock of my heart?

Who gave you the code to open the door?
Did you pick up the key where it lay on the floor?

Was it winter or summer, autumn or spring
When our pie full of blackbirds started to sing?

Did it snow, did it rain from the heavens above
When the weather was altered for ever by love?

Tell me the story; what did I do
In the darkest of ages before there was you?

How did we live when the world wasn't us;
Did we sit with a book at the back of the bus?

Did we go to the pub and let out guffaws
At the unfunny jokes of impossible bores?

How did we manage before there was love
And the two of us met like a hand in a glove?

Tell me the story; where could we be
Except in this world of you and of me?

OF EARTH, WATER, AIR AND FIRE

Aardvark

Avidly, all alphabets aspire to A1 precedence:
builders and bodgers, chippies and chasers,
eager to head the weekly paper's small-ads list.

And so this prehistoric-seeming beast,
with long protruding nose, plump tail,
and fondness for the dark,

goes burrowing in the night-time bush
for ant and termite, unaware of its symbolic life
as tradesman's Number One.

The God of the Egyptians took your shape;
and from your teeth the Hausa magic-men make charms
against the failings of the heart.

Lizard

Gone quick as thought:
a shiver, a sliver of speed,
a dart and dive into a crack;
no dust raised, no trace left.

Here's an older one
wrinkled, fat and green,
whose leathery fuselage,
pants in the morning sun.

A flicked tongue tests
for airborne food;
eyes gleam, undeceived and
narrowed to the main chance.

Enough! This lumbering ancient
turns and slithers down
a slanted slab of marble,
baking to the touch.

Orang-Utan

We tense at each collision
as you strike the bars.

Those orange wisps of fur,
the bruised, black nose,

the eyes that plead
as if I held the keys

that could release you
from this narrow cage.

Badger

Tenacious, stubborn, driving forward in the dark,
no obstacle allowed to block his path,
a tough exemplum of the single mind.

But he's no match for the confusing lights
that sweep around the bend at midnight,
dazzled, displaced, quickly dispatched.

At dawn, stiff paws and bloodied muzzle
rigid beneath a hawthorn hedge:
the grey, the white, the darkened red.

Vole

Small forager and fossicker
beneath a drift of leaf;
twitching snout alert
for food, ears to danger,
fine whiskers pricked,
dark bright eyes alive:

a dainty dish to set before an owl.

Tortoises

Along the ancient Way,
between the grave reliefs
and tumbled stone,
their speed surprises us.

The green is dotted
with dried turds,
slight wisps of shrivelled black
they've left behind as calling-cards.

A wrinkled neck peeps out
from armour-plating
into which (at fear or dudgeon)
it will suddenly withdraw.

They've made this place their fief,
their park and pleasure-ground,
know where the ribboned stream
and luscious grasses are.

Kerameikos Cemetery, Athens

Kangaroo

Driving at night, a country road,
I hear a knock or thump,
that darkness can't identify

and once again
I feel guilt's tremor,
its sourness in my veins;

recall, two decades past,
a thundering coach
in Queensland;

the same dull smack
that flicked the "roo"
into the roadside dark.

The driver joked,
we settled back to sleep's
unsettled dreams.

Hedgehogs

A hedgehog family, mid-afternoon,
shuffling and circling on the lawn;
small spiked balls in the maternal field.

Surely darkness is their proper sphere;
the long, nocturnal work beneath the hedge
among the rustling, crackling leaves.

Out here in sunlight we inspect
their prickled rumps, turned to us
with polite (or impolite) indifference.

They are absorbed with grass
and have no time for protocols of light,
or prohibitions of the clock.

Lambs

. . . it is as if it were the earth that flung them, not themselves . . .
– Gerard Manley Hopkins

Teenaged gangs, rowdy at the field's corner,
they go in packs, racing and leaping
in the chill, late light of March.

It is 'blackthorn weather': deceiving sun
soon making way for cold
as the flame leaps in the grate.

Their stoic parents, like the aged without teeth,
munch with loose jaws, and lazy eyes
take all this in: the cries, the frisky jumps.

They will return when they need something
but for now the electric shock of new life
prods them, with a buzz, into the bright air.

Leech

You have a right to live.
Even the blood-sucker
crawling up my leg
deserves a life: discuss!

The jungle walk
becomes a battle
with your insistence
on the taste of blood.

Later, two helpful boys,
Chinese Malay, suggest
a leaf of brown tobacco
has power to staunch the flow;

they hand it on a thumb,
like a craftsman in gold-leaf,
delicately laying down
a shimmer, a fragile gleam.

Taman Negara National Park

Bear

The quiet civility of chess
absorbs Sofia's central park,
the players wordlessly absorbed.

Light early summer air:
new flowers, girls in groups
flirt with the nervous boys.

The noise of an accordion:
a glum and ragged bear
led forward on a chain.

His master orders coffee,
yawns, and yanks the chain;
business is bad – the world and its compassion!

Someone must suffer: let it be the bear.
Who at the next pull staggers up
and claps his dirty paws.

Eel

It's a moon thing,
the private temper of the eel;
we cannot penetrate
arcana of the shallows:

the moment when instinct turns
towards Sargasso,
and the call of reproduction
(with concomitant dying) starts.

Like a child's scribble
with a fat black crayon
they skitter through the pool,
clouding its gravel bottom.

Blunt heads but sharp teeth,
like those of the long pike
that fasten on the skin
with terrible tenacity.

Toad

A leather armchair, wrinkled and distressed,
deep, suspect folds of muddy brown,
in which all kinds of slime inhere.

Hunkered in your damp corner, under leaves,
somnolent: the disturbed, reluctant clamber
when I wake you from your sleep, says all.

You carry the burden of your reputation;
old poets had you down as metaphor
of all-sized loathsomeness: cold toad.

Indeed, but if I spoke who'd care to listen?
How counter such inveterate prejudice
that draws a moral from our body's form?

Why should the beautiful possess the earth?
and natural ugliness make us loathed,
the ones whom accident or genes make foul?

I have the last laugh, here in my soft bed,
in a dank place where I'm not disturbed;
I sleep while you rush round in endless toil!

Wagtail

The wagtail freezes
as if, just then, it has
retrieved a lost idea
then, having thought, moves on,
its tail an aircraft-guider's bat
conveying some message,
or only up-and-down, up-and-down,

scattering itself across the road,
pattering the tarmac of the lane,
quick curves and fast-paced trots,
whiter than white with touch of grey –

my morning gift, a grace gratuitous.

Kingfisher

Are rarities the best?
The sudden swoop of blue
above this sluggish river
where a bulbous nest hangs
like a lantern from a branch,
inviolable, apart,
as camera lenses close.

The tourist boat, itself no rarity,
glides softly on the Styx
and we obey the rite
of taking water
from the steersman's scoop:
our pores drink immortality,
we emulate the gods.

Jackdaws

Circling the twin towers of Rhuddlan castle.
as if their dance were choreographed,
jackdaws scream in the fresh wind.

(In school we'd draw these cylinders,
sketching the nibbled foot stone-robbers left
after a night of furtive work.)

Only a smear of white on the cold steps,
a brief caw as they climb,
define their fleeting, shorthold tenancy.

Pelican

We know, and you know,
who's Boss and *numero uno:*
the guy who swaggers,
who Mick Jaggers.

Look at that bald coot,
hardly visible in the shoot;
hasn't a chance to shine,
to speak even one line,

pecking the dirt
in his black shirt,
while you just gloat
over that great pink throat,

and the enormous beak
which is the peak
attraction, igniting sparks
in the Royal Parks.

Like an 'S' hook,
we follow the crook
of your distinctive shape
from webbed feet to nape

and that sexy tuft's
the sort of thing that Cruft's
would reward in a poodle.
You're a child's doodle.

Stilts

Never a better name: *échelle élégante*,
stylishly stalking the shallow waters
of the salt marsh at Hyères.

Catwalk sleek, on thinnest legs,
they are our substitute for the *flamants*
too busy at their nests just now to flaunt

their pinkness at the curious passer-by;
so we're content with stilts, lowering their heads
to pluck the flat salt pools.

Just like those clowns at Billy Smart's,
who strode in stripey trousers, grinning down
as children stepped between their swaying legs.

Jaculus

O who has heard of the jaculus,
the flying serpent that leaps on us?

Lucan and Pliny and Isodore
include it in their animal store.

Their bestiary-bibles all record,
like a javelin or poisoned sword,

a drone, unpiloted, whose fiery breath
deals in the currency of instant death:

out of the sky a savage dart
that stops the motions of the heart.

Swan

On Hindwell Pool the swan is buried in itself,
then lifts its neck to stare through darkened brows.

Conscious of magnificence, that stately glide
asserts possession of the tree-screened pool.

When at Old Radnor bells peal out,
the neolithic Stones break ranks,

lost chiefs once turned to weathered stone
remember who they were, and walk

to slake their thirst, swan or no swan,
at the waters of this freezing pond.

Last day of April, sunlight chasing frost,
the swan's neck rears, alone in pride.

Pheasant

That rough squawk from the windbox,
then the flap of beating wings:

no one likes to be disturbed,
least of all this gaudy racer.

Fond of the ground, of verge and tarmac,
its end comes quickly with a bumper-scuffle.

Later, I come home to find a brace
hung on pink twine from my cottage door:

a neighbour's gift, well-meant.
But I'm a reluctant butcher,

plucking feathers in a cloudy whirl,
drawing that stew of guts and grain

still undigested in the belly's bag,
to toss in a bucket with the rest.

So much blood and stink, such disarray
for one brief meal of roasted game:

breast cage collapsed, like a ruined church,
its arches broken, jutting all which way.

Crow

There's something unappealing in that walk,
an arrogance, a cold rapacity
high on the reek of blood.

You bring to mind the air of A
who edits *The Usual Suspects*
where X reviews the latest Y

who sat on that prize-giving team
which gave the palm to X
(who handed it with grace to Y

the back end of the year before).
And round it goes, the pecking beak
that pulls at yellow entrails

smeared with red, a pretty mess
streaking the tarmac, till a car's
approaching whine sends up a flap of wings.

Ibis

Eater of snakes in the old beast-books:
corpse-lover, shirker of the purifying font,
waiting for carrion at the water's edge.

With that hooked bill you might do anything,
fishing and foraging the simplest task
for a wader armed with such a piece of kit.

But they saw you as a diner on flesh,
shunning the spirit's banquet; with a nasty habit
of wiping your arse with what that beak scooped up.

Owl

Does that look express
vexation at the metaphor
we force upon you?

Wise owl, but why?
Does fierce rigidity
on that short branch,

a baleful eye,
a prudent silence,
a coldly swivelled neck,

imply that garrulous,
quick syllables,
redundant noise

are faults of ours,
scuffling in the grass
and shrubs beneath?

But later, in the dark,
the rapid hoot,
the cry, a scream,

disclose that you, like us,
cannot resist the lure
of grabbing what you can.

Robin

Perched on the spade's handle
you seem ready for a question.

The intent eyes gleam, the song trills
but nothing is given away.

You sing in winter light,
hop lightly on your perch.

This could mean the start of dialogue;
I clear my throat, lean forward.

Then a flap and sudden dart
through the gapped thorn of a frozen hedge.

Phoenix

Don't give me that!
Measure this hokum
by the girl who sits
(the plastic drum of ashes
pinned between her knees)
in silence on the high speed train.

She's come to scatter
on the ravaged mountain side
(where the slag heaps
strive to mount a flower-show
above the pithead wheels)
his petal-light and airy residue.

Salamander

Cool customer of fire,
the godly needed you as proof
that righteous souls survive the holocaust.

When you have climbed inside
the canopy of apple-blossom,
every bitten fruit can kill.

Sinister, this chill immunity,
this furnace-freedom,
exempt from passion's heat.

By contrast, we are basted
in the flame and crackle
of the purging pyre,

the one that melts us like a slick
of rubber tyre turned liquid black:
no chance of second thought, remorse.

TRENCH FEET

1

Jeremy Button, bright as his name,
clever, well-favoured, at the top of his game,
sits at the laptop at a quarter to three,
confronting the question: and what about *Me*?

Emma from History's got her own show:
The Suffragette Struggle, blow by damned blow,
but help is at hand, for the year is '14 –
The First World War Poets just right for the screen.

Jo Gilbert's a treasure and put in a word,
during dinner at Oxford with Anthony Bird,
commissioning giant of BBC Four,
who owed her a favour (but let's not say more).

A meeting was called at St George's Hotel
which went, as it happened, surprisingly well.
Before they had even completed the soup,
Jeremy Button was spliced in the loop.

And off Jerry cantered, his stallion snorting,
impatient to start on the archival sorting:
O, greatcoats and duckboards, ponies and rats,
poppies and skeletons, mud and tin hats!

Where to begin on these fabulous riches?
But, quick, before others compete with their pitches
(rumour's now ended the well-kept trade mystery
of Channel 4's coup: *A Soldier's Gay History*).

No time, now, to squander; he needs a good team
(Miranda, the graduate student, a dream:
she'll do it for nothing, quite happy to earn
the wages of zero as the show's new 'intern').

There'll be articles, too, in *Guardian Weekend*
and plenty of cash in the coffers to spend
on outfits and lunches, permissions and rights,
and Jerry has Faber cross-lined in his sights.

Simply nothing can fail, and bang on her cue,
the Laureate stands to deliver the view
that the poets were victims, their generals malign.
Yet 'Englishness' glistens in every last line.

2

The first day of shooting (with a clutter of vans,
mobile *cantinas*, dropped litter and cans)
and across the flat fields, like peaceable waves
the soft undulation of thousands of graves.

Just outside Arras, where Rosenberg lies
Jerry's adjusting his brightest of ties
that flames like the stubble when harvest is done.
Now far in the West the diminishing sun

composes the drop for the opening shot:
the tear-jerking starter that gives us the lot:
O, greatcoats and duckboards, ponies and rats,
poppies and skeletons, mud and tin hats!

Who cares if the critics are queueing to slate it,
or listing mags fail in their duty to rate it?
Let the internet trolls fire their whizz-bangs of bile,
the deals have been done, and that trade-mark sweet smile

of Jerry on camera, in dugout and ditch,
deflects the assault of that 'maudlin kitsch'
a critic has pasted across the first screening,
(with 'talentless', 'facile', 'spiteful', 'left-leaning').

The first of the poems, the victor ludorum,
is Owen's explosive 'Dulce et Decorum'
(with Thomas's 'Easter' and Rosenberg's rat
runners-up in this opening race of the flat).

News comes that the orders, in spite of the flak,
are coming to Amazon, Kindle – and a stack
at each old-fashioned bookstore: a lift to the hearts
of a range of ambitious and tweedy old farts

who rush out their tie-ins and timely reprints,
each vying for airtime and festival stints.
At Hay-on-Wye's tents, in a Flanders-like field,
the book lovers queue for clichés to be wheeled,

like a groaning field cannon on clay-spattered wheels,
to position and whoosh! like those black-and-white reels
they flicker the news (none had worked out before?):
men died or were maimed in a horrible War.

3

The ante is upped, the *Mail* now fights back
a predictable Minister's on the attack.
Jerry's fetched to the studio's intimate circle,
squeezed between Weather and Angela Merkel.

'Jeremy Button, the Minister's right,
is he not, that your view of the conflict is trite:
with donkeys in charge and lions chewed up?
We've heard it before: the generals screwed up.'

With the sweetest of smiles, Jerry looks at the screen
where Montague Smith from Westminster is beamed:
'It's more complex than *he*' (with a sneer on his lips)
'concludes from your very tendentious short clips.

Historians do battle in seminar rooms
yet no firm conclusion from all of it looms;
the jury is out, the facts are disputed.
Mr Smith, in the past, cited 'facts' when it suited,

but now is pursuing his well-known vendetta
against all who want to make the world better,
viz. "the Left" in his words, utopian dreamers,
peaceniks and herbivores, Trotskyite schemers.

His passion for war,' Jerry takes a deep breath,
'not shared by his grandad who, rather than death,
chose to scurry to Sweden in Nineteen Sixteen
when conscription confronted the average teen.'

'Outrageous! Contemptible!' spluttered the Tory,
who'd gone to great lengths to stifle this story
that Jerry's researchers had emailed at speed,
to his BBC taxi with the strapline: MUST READ!

A cheap shot of course, but the stakes were now high,
for rumours were coming that the Chinese would buy
a subtitled version of Jeremy's chronicle,
that showed how the West was inept and quite comical.

The anchor now smiled, the producer was pleased,
as the link to Frau Merkel was tactfully eased
and Jerry withdrew from the studio, thanked,
by a low-paid assistant who suddenly yanked

from her handbag a contract and took him downstairs
where the taxi was waiting, the driver's shrewd stares
becoming: 'Was you on that thing on the box
abaht the Great War; those poor, flipping Jocks.

Slaughter it was, we treat cattle better.
We've still got at home my old granddad's letter
he sent to my grandma the day that he died...'
'Drop me here, that's just fine,' Jerry expertly lied.

4

Great news that the tie-in, its triumph assured
is now on the shortlist for the highest award.
The sponsors from FidoFine, rather on edge,
stand in a cluster like sheep by a hedge.

Dog meat providers in stiff business suits
they're estranged from the writers who seem in cahoots.
So this is the truth of a book awards party;
the joshing and sloshing of the top literati:

The boys in spiked hair and neatly pressed shirts
and the girls with their trays, in tiny black skirts
ogled by portly old geezers who paw
as they leer and stretch out their glasses for more.

The canapés tiny and light and absurd
are swallowed in gulps – as a predatory bird
would swoop on a creature and gobble it straight;
used cocktail-sticks plaintively wave for a plate.

'Jerry,' bawls Richard from his knot by the door.
'Come meet Araminta; you know her, I'm sure.'
They approach and are canny as old lovers are,
wary, ironic, polite from afar.

'Araminta informs me,' pompous Dick starts to spiel,
'that you're favourite tonight and the Poundrite, I feel,
is likewise assured. This boy's on a roll,'
he confides as fat fingers feel at a bowl

of olives, unpitted, which soon set up strife
in the wreck of his teeth and he calls for his wife
who runs with a handkerchief, dabbing his gums,
impatiently scolding: 'They're worse than your Mum's.'

'For God's sake!' spits Arrie, 'That man is a fright.
He's slimy when sober and revolting when tight.'
'I agree,' Jerry smiles, relieved to discover
a common terrain with his handsome ex-lover.

Did I make a mistake? he starts to reflect,
but before he can speak the girls interject:
'The dinner is served, please move to your table.'
A simple instruction, but some poets, unstable,

totter forward and stumble and crash to the floor,
helped up by their comrades still eager for more:
they seize all the bottles and build a stockade
to sustain them until the announcement is made.

Unpublished, unfêted, unpaid, unreviewed,
their egos alone unimpaired in the feud
between Talent and Money, where whatever they write
puts them up with the angels, pure Art, divine light.

At the end there are speeches and the warmest applause
when it's Jerry who takes it, Jerry of course.
The pieces are written, the eulogies done,
the snappers all get him, he was bound to have won.

Next day he is shocked to be tweeted a link
to the *Mail* where foul Monty has raised quite a stink.
The jury was nobbled, he seems to imply;
revenge is the motive; 'Touché!' Monty's cry.

TV DON AND HIS LOVER, CHAIR OF THE JUDGES.
A headline that offers no get-outs or fudges:
Araminta's sweet smile, hand in hand on the pier,
judge, jury, and sentence for Jerry, that's clear.

The pic's five years old but that's a mere fact
and no one is troubled, the point is: that pact,
of sexual congress and favours returned
(no point in riposting love's boat is long burned).

Jerry's face in his hands, he slumps on the sofa
to watch it unravel: old footage, a gopher
he sacked coyly feeding the flickering flames
with accounts of their trysting, and naming of names.

The day of his triumph, the series now ending,
and on Twitter his love life the sole thing that's trending.
The weeks out in Flanders (or Notting Hill Gate
in a studio editing eight until eight)

All wasted, all shattered the hall of his dreams
where only the statuette mockingly gleams.
The War should have made him, the award clinched the deal,
acclaim, money, honours from the very first reel.

The year was for him, his the subject, the hour
but now he has blown it and everything's sour:
O, greatcoats and duckboards, ponies and rats,
poppies and skeletons, mud and tin hats!

THE SECRETS OF THE SEA

Walk

En quoi un homard est-il plus ridicule qu'un chien, qu'un chat, qu'une gazelle,
qu'un lion ou toute autre bête dont on se fait suivre? J'ai le goût des homards,
qui sont tranquilles, sérieux, savent les secrets de la mer, n'aboient pas . . .
– Words attributed to Gérard de Nerval by Théophile Gautier

I see Nerval coaxing his lobster,
on a leash of blue ribbon.
He has made his case
for preference of pet:
because it does not bark
and knows the secrets of the sea.

In this morning's market
the great crustaceans twitch;
a pair of claws squeezes the air;
liquid eels in slippery ranks
slither on stainless steel;
a salmon sleeps in a drift of ice.

Those bloody aprons,
that pink tump of guts
coiled like a frivolous dessert,
enforce a preference for
the *Bois* – poet and *homard*,
like a pair of lovers, hand in hand.

Whaling Museum, Pico Island

It's just us, in this whip of wind and water:
December in the Azores, blown
from the jetty where they would haul them in.

We seek for refuge among iron vats
where they melted hacked blubber.
Crude, long-handled blades

now lean against the walls, unemployed
but visible on the flickering loop of film,
where the hunters are running

like part-time firemen from their fields,
triggered by the alarm, the whale spouting,
giving itself away, the light boats racing.

Then bones ground to flour, sperm oil tapped,
everything chopped and fired and milled,
not a sliver or chip, not a tooth of it wasted.

Annotations of Byzantium

1

I am woman and you call me names:
circus dancer, whore, magician . . . Empress.

Beneath my chamber, secret tunnels run
where men are shut to waste or die;

where night dissolves in day like powders
losing presence in a lethal glass.

They wander in the dark, go mad, lose sight;
I tether them like cattle to a manger

where they feed, a rope around the neck,
who thought they could resist my power.

This I do for Antonina, consort of Belisarius,
the man who cowers while she slakes her lust

with Theodosius, the Thracian boy;
I am woman; I know need and strength.

2

Beneath the dome of Wisdom,
coming from shadows, we greet the patriarch.

Look at our work, great canopy of stone,
mathematics of magnificence.

Later, the salt sea whips my cheeks;
the wind streaks madly from the Dardanelles,

nature and art in passionate contention
where I award, between them both, the prize.

3

He is in the marshes, hunting crane,
watching the violent beat of wings,

patient to cripple the great, beautiful bird
that rises in the mellow light of dawn.

4

They shall say that Theodora rose
'from humble origin', lap-dancer

in the royal eye, to take the purple;
add in 'whore', for it's desire

that frightens them, the narrowed eye,
the jewelled goblet raised and aimed,

a rustle in the chamber's passage
where a curtain billows, candle flame

trembles excitedly at what it sees;
lips sealed by willing servitude.

Island

Brendan's monks have lit a fire
where gutted fish brown on whittled sticks,
and God is thanked for the air of a small island.

There is no hint of what's to come:
the slide of embers, the tilt and scatter,
when the whale lifts itself from seeming sleep.

The Secrets of the Sea

A great shoal of underwater photographers,
trailing plumes of bubbles, track
the ghostly path of sharks, catch
the striped magnificence of fish.

A wristwatch tapped, a clumsy mime
to distant colleagues in their masks;
a finger points into the gloom:
a ray flaps its ancient cloak,

the small fry scatter, and the wrasse's eye
turns in slow disgust
on the limber frog men with false feet.
They work at cataloguing marvels:

what finally evades them is the secret life
of the observed, the enigmatic eye
that watches men, ungainly in the deep,
struggle behind their walls of glass.

The Forge

Hopkins in Liverpool, 1880

After the rain, in scanty sun-glitter,
wind whips up from the river,
and the shy priest steps into the dark
where the farrier, Felix, labours,

the hoof in a skilled grip,
at his patient ministry of shoeing;
the heavy draught horse shifts,
and the drayman quips in the flamelight.

Bright at the back there, the forge
glows from its fell of steep coals;
old nails gleam on the earth floor,
and the silent man is hardly noticed,

felt hat in his hand, his collar
a ring of whiteness, intent eye
marking the chiaroscuro, hearing
the hammer and ring of hard trade.

In this theatre of darkness
and flickering forge-light,
the two of them labour
in a difficult silence.

Innocence

I shot at a great Bird which I saw sitting upon a Tree on the Side of a great Wood, I believe it was the first Gun that had been fir'd there since the Creation of the World.
– Defoe, *Robinson Crusoe*

With the echo of that shot,
the upward beat of wings,
something stained the silence
that could not be scrubbed out.

The man in a shaggy cap
and a patchwork of animal skins
shot off through the undergrowth,
muttering to his beard:

My priority cannot be undone
nor my knowledge of musket and ball,
the cask of dry powder, pistols,
the toolkit of death.

What can I do with such knowledge?
Like liquor spilled on the sand
from the stoppered flask,
I watch it trickle and stain.

After this the footprint,
the certainty of Others,
the slow unspooling
and the not going back.

Too late for regrets:
the sprung Jack has leapt
from the opened box;
the genie has slipped from the bottle.

Lost Time

I could have crept into any alderman's thumb-ring . . .
– Falstaff

Ah, the thickening, the slow expansion,
like rising dough on a warm board.

I was the skinny athlete of that family snap
breasting the tape, hands raised, victor.

But that was an old song: so sing a new one,
a song of change, of the not-what-has-been,

but what surprises us on a fresh morning
in the cold, undeceiving heart of winter:

the glitter of frost, a wagtail wandering
and skittering on the white dance-floor,

dragging its partner, that obedient tail.

Helmet

In a French *brocante,*
I see a diver's helmet,
its copper and brass
massive and marvellous;
the fine-threaded bolts
denuded of their nuts.

Last seen at the Pier Head,
when the child watched
as they dipped a diver
in the blackness of the dock;
felt the fear seeing him
vanish in that spaceman's suit.

Later, I was appeased
by a bath-time replica.
In his plastic suit of grey
he sent up bubbles
when I blew into a tube:
his urgent proof and sign of life.

Cushions

I think of Hans Christian Andersen,
and that troll's feast inside the mountain.

The glittering, illusory people
sat down on dark, luxurious cushions

which were revealed as black mice,
nibbling at each other's tails.

I think of it, watching the voles,
scurrying into the cracks

of a stone wall, so fleet, and light
upon the earth.

Glint

'Were I not Alexander I would be Diogenes'
– Alexander the Great, having granted Diogenes his request that
he move out of his light

Alexander the all-powerful,
happy to grant the wisdom
of the barrel-haunting sage,   ˙
to concede his sagacity of denial,
his intelligent taste for the frugal.

But not so far as to relinquish
the great, gilt crown,
that catches the sun
from a high window,
glinting its confidence.

The Trouble with Epitaphs

They work through chiselled cold
when warmth of life, moist breath,
are what I'd like to see epitomised.

I'd have the mason cut a keener font
to catch the lovely sharpness
of a dung-spread field in March;

the bright gleam on an empty road
after a fierce, short drench of rain;
bright air where mild hills interlock.

Inscribe a text for me that lives,
unlike this mossy epitaph I trace
with a finger's darkening tip.

THE MIGRANT SHIP

The Voyage Out

Pot-bellied sails, a lively wind, then off.
Our 'loved ones' on the slippery quay,
unsure of what their weeping proves.

After three months, our landfall at Utopia,
the island that imagination made,
the not-a-place that lacks the usual flaws.

That it would fail and break apart
like the scattered carcass of an egg
the stay-at-homes predicted well.

But did they know the whipped breeze,
the first roof raised, the marvellous bird
that carols to us from a jutting bough?

The Migrant Ship

1

We were too many:
crowded to the rail,
as the quay abandoned us;
water widened.

Don't ask if fear or hope,
drove us in the first days;
don't ask what thoughts
skittered in our heads;

just say we wondered
how long our food would last,
how we might face the heat
of that stinking hold.

2

I spread them on my cloth:
a tiny elephant of brass,
a ring, a ball of glass,
a silver box containing nothing.

3

The boy with the lazy eye
each morning carved a notch
on a stick with a red tassel;
we shunned his tally

having no need
of such knowledge
as the days drifted us
out of reach of time.

4

Each had his own moment
when the darkness entered
into a personal silence
no one else could share.

I cannot tell you its smell,
bitter taste on the tongue,
the longing to retch
when the stomach is empty.

It was the knowledge of nothing:
that the ship's motion,
which should take us forward,
was infinite regression.

90

5

I was sleeping when the cries started.
I woke to a panic on the hot deck;
the engines silent and the crew cursing
as the vessel slumped, a sick beast.

One by one we dropped to the water
– boys in a river pool splashing –
but no shore neared,
no watchers called a warning.

Some sank without striving,
others, treading the water,
inspected the ocean,
its taciturn vastness.

6

When the boats came out
from the sleeping island
they handled us harshly,
shouting in anger

in a strange language.
They hauled us up roughly
over the harsh side,
the ones who were left.

7

I remember the stillness
as we entered the harbour,
how the gulls cried
from the stone quayside.

I remember the silence,
the fishermen's faces
lifted towards us
as they sorted their catches.

I remember my yearning
for the comfort of sleep
where I hoped to forget
the need for this journey.

I remember the box
that I felt for with fingers
that knew its hinged lid
opened on nothing.

Calais

This mud is different.
Were I writing home
I'd struggle to describe
its darker pigment,
how it slips beneath our feet,
a long, slow slide
where boots lose grip.

Under our sheeting
we listen to the rain;
traffic on the near road
lets out a groan, a hiss.
We have learned the art
of slow patience,
of being still, endlessly.

There is always tomorrow,
always the chance
that there will be movement.
Today we cheered
when someone's phone
showed a man walking
out of a tunnel's darkness.

Acrobat

Now you see me;
now you don't.

That backward flip
that leaves me standing,

and the crowd gasping,
is just for show.

Inside, I'm still;
I haven't moved an inch.

Here on this beach
at the Atlantic coast

fear leaps in my heart,
turns somersault,

in a trick presented
for my private ring.

I am lean and fit
because I rarely eat.

It is not dread of fall
clenches my heart,

Go on, watch this,
as I leap to the shoulder

of my brother
who is not my brother:

the one I abandoned
in the salt dark.

Carpe Diem

Now pluck and snip, cut off and clip
the rose that slips its tight green sheath,
like someone drawing down a zip,
to step into a nakedness that holds

what also dies.

There is no point of rest, no stay.
Perfection is a flash of light;
it sniffs the odour of decay,
so catch it while it flies.

Attention

This is an interesting planet.
It deserves all the attention you can give it.
– Marilynne Robinson, *Gilead*

Don't worry, you have my attention;

I can hear the soft knock of a beak
tapping under my eaves.

I can see the valley slipping out of mist.
I can feel the warmth of sunned stone.
I can taste the sharpness of a pippin
I can smell the cracked piths of a flailed hedge.

It is this world and no other world;
it is no simulacrum, no notion or idea,
no construct of the mind but is itself
in all its passionate clarity.

So, for this reason, you have my attention.

A Green Thought

She dreams of foliage:
how finger-stems
hold breaking buds;
a crimson crown.

Her body wrapped
in sticky goose-grass,
the odour of her skin
cool as dank moss.

She takes her lover
by the hand to teach
a dozen ways
of tenderness

and lies with him
beneath new canopies
where light flickers
and earth stirs.

Her skin's sheen
smooth as a chestnut
in its spiny case
where it lies like a violin.

Pungent as wild garlic,
or the warm soil
after a short drench,
she is fecund, eager,

riding the thermals
of her dream
across the sky of night,
chary of waking.

Riddles

1

You admire my tall neck,
that seems to promise pleasure.
No invitation to caress.
Not loved for itself,
but for what it admits
into the space between us.

A sound in my throat
anticipates, like desire,
what is to come,
as I let myself release
in a quick, short dash
an acrid, if interesting, scent.

2

Rectangle of admirable simplicity,
it has the power to remove
all trace of error, to cancel
all our compounded faults.

A sacrament of absolution,
making the soul white,
restoring its first state
of shimmering innocence

in a motion we doubt,
having been this way before,
tottering with a whoop
on the loose stones of the path.

The Unwritten Love Poems

If they are absent,
or not copious,
I blame the hours
that we have spent;

I mean months and years
lived with no provident
gathering and stacking
of seasoned logs in store

but warming our hands,
wastefully, at the flame
of an improvised blaze
made out of driftwood.

The Quizzicock

I fabricate a bird,
whose brilliant plumage
foxes the ornithologist,
(the one with a green vest
of many pockets).

He hugs binoculars
to his verdant chest
and whistles slowly
through gapped teeth,
cocks his ear to the sound

my new flyer makes
as it dips from a fir
with a flash of crimson,

blue, white, and gold;
prodigal in its dash,

knowing itself sublime,
too quick to let itself
acquire our admiration.
The quizzicock
crying in the trees,

waiting to be classified,
fitted in, pinned down.
But first a squawk
and upward dart,
glitter of that gold.

Kite

A kite and crow
contest the sky,
like flying aces.

They do not know
the end's foregone,
as in all rigged races.

These feints and swoops,
this mimic violence,
are just a show:

such desperate loops
and air-show tricks,
watched from below,

confirm the strong
at their old game
of hammering the weak.

Though crowds may throng
and bookies thrive,
The victor has the sharpest beak.

Capital

I

I manage funds,
I make wealth grow;
a peasant in her fields
watching the eggplant swell,
knows what I know,
the gift of munificence.

I am monarch of gold,
delving my hands
into the chest of coin,
feeling its hardness
in my palms, its sliding mass
like pebbles on a beach.

How hateful the poor,
with their low horizons,
their fear of risk;
they envy us who make
all that they possess,
as gods may light the sky.

II

The Lord is not in this house,
said Ambrose the saint
when the tycoon bragged

of his infinite riches,
of his claim to possess
absolute happiness.

Then the earth opened
and swallowed his abundance
in a cloud of dust.

All this the saint observed
with a backward look,
as he ran with his companion.

A DOG'S BREXIT

1

Who'd be a dog in England now?
They patronize my suffering brow
    with soft caress.
Sometimes I snatch my bone and race
    into some dark, secluded place
    unable to remain at home and face
        this rottenness.

Let me, a hound with drooping ears, dissent
    from all that yapping rabblement
        of loud MPs
so that a calmer, canine view prevails
    above the shrill, discordant wails
    of Members as each tries (and fails)
        to please.

Which part of 'exit' did you miss?
    constituency parties hiss
        at those
    too frightened to assert,
    that cutting loose will hurt
more than it heals (as every Jacques and Kurt
        well knows).

A noxious vapour reaches overseas,
    borne on a toxic, xenophobic breeze
        of hate.
And friends abroad, whose own Far Right
    grows eager for a matching fight,
        predict a European night.
            Too late!

My hide's a mellow shade of whisky,
my temper's generally frisky
but not today
as I look out at public life,
its raucous noise and vapid strife,
where trolls and tweeters wield the knife
and say:

Hard Brexit now! Let Parliament not decide!
Give Albion back its ancient pride.
Enough's enough!
Don't get me wrong, it's not migration
but love of our great British nation
that fuels our blazing indignation . . .
'Woof! Woof!'

I cannot hold my barking back
hearing their tongues' redundant clack.
Dishonest prattle!
We want our country back, they cry
who handed it to tax-avoiding, fly,
globetrotting firms not shy
of battle

with mere governments – or workers
flung like Christians in the circus
to lions' jaws.
Relishing the terror-cries of pain,
they judge all protest to be vain;
claim total freedom to disdain
our laws.

My vegan mistress is so sweet,
she feeds me plates of bleeding meat
until I moan
contentedly with stretched out paws
while on the TV someone jaws
about the need to make our laws
our own.

But all those 'Brits' with properties in France
now rush to join this village dance
and rail
at 'Brussels bureaucrats' –but grasp too late
that health care costs can escalate
when you've said bonne nuit to the Eurostate.
The *Daily Mail*

(much read where sun-soaked expats crowd)
sends out its message clear and loud
each day:
this is your chance to get your country back
so don't believe that righteous claque
of liberal leftist journos; keep on track
with Mrs May.

She'll see off courts of human rights,
the health-and-safety law that blights
our antique land.
Like bold Britannia with her spear
she'll bond with Trump, and engineer
a future countless nations fear
is built on sand.

In Strasbourg, Farage and his MEPs,
waxed fat on all their doles and fees
(like geese
who guzzle in the dirt for scraps),
with a bunch of City finance chaps
(gobs fastened to the barrel taps)
thought up a wheeze

(a common one in politics) to have it all;
to do one thing and then to call
for its obverse.
While feeding greedily from gourmet plates
set out enticingly by Far Right mates
(pausing to photo-call with pints of Thwaites)
they curse

the trough from which they slurp,
denounce 'fat cats' then burp,
replete.
Back at the Hilton, on the king-size bed,
the latest heap of Euro cash is spread.
They're clothed in bling from head
to feet.

Their party's tiny, a sad rump
but much beloved by Donald Trump,
the troll,
who shares a preference for their crude
pub politics: as subtle as an over-stewed
lunch platter mopped up with a chewed
bread roll.

When I was rescued from the pound
where fifty dogs made such a sound
all night
sleep seemed a hopeless choice
I thought that humans spoke with softer voice
but now *Today in Parliament*'s wild noise
has put me right.

But when a predator has got your scent
you know that solidarity makes sense
if you'd survive.
The sheep don't see the wolf as friend,
'listening' to grievances, smiling without end.
Faced with such cant their instincts blend
to stay alive!

It's true some dogs exploit their owners,
like opera houses flattering donors
for more;
but even they must sometimes pause to ask,
'What if they're not quite equal to the task?'
It's then you'll see the slipping mask,
the naked claw

rip up a cheek which once was patted;
the much-loved pet now kicked not flattered:
get lost!
as false friends knife you from behind,
forgetting all those tender, kind
deceitful words that from a weasel mind
they tossed.

Some truths from me, your barking chum,
who's not, in spite of what it seems, so dumb
or lacking sense.
The first is that the world belongs to those
who have the power to impose
their moneyed will, whose every instinct flows
towards that end.

So I'm not sold on all that pious talk
that columnists and preachers hawk
ad infinitum.
I'd rather trust my nature as a hunter
who doesn't waffle, spout or chunter.
They squeal like your plump Billy Bunter
when mongrels bite 'em.

Yet still, some things are hard for dogs
to fathom. Like the creaking cogs
that haul
a mountain rack-and-pinion train
we pull at every portion of our brain
but after all that heave and strain
we simply stall.

It makes no sense: your brandished ballot box
whose outcome regularly mocks
its boast
to be the people's voice (that bravely checks
the State) when too few bother to scratch 'X'.
It's honest as a fist of dodgy cheques,
or banker's toast.

Your PM, May, the vicar's daughter
was voted for by just below a quarter.
The people's will!
Don't make me laugh! The populists now say
that 'disillusioned' voters come their way;
but watch their back-door bagmen pay
the bill

of media moguls, commentators, trolls,
by whose assistance (helped by dodgy polls)
they're elected,
their promises soon sent to landfill in a cart;
the 'disillusioned' worth a tinker's fart,
these demagogues whose poisoned heart
's infected.

I'd rather see a pack of my wild mates
pissing against their garden gates
than this:
the cant of caring, 'listening' to the bleats
of those they've coached to blame 'élites',
engage class war from comfy seats
that hiss

when lazy bums collapse in them to zap
the channels or consult an app:
a dog's life!
Anything but fight as their ancestors fought
for what they felt was right and sought
to gain through common action and who taught
through strife.

8

Through battles that you fight in solidarity
with others who perceive with equal clarity
the fact
that finding scapegoats, pinning blame
on immigrants whose lives are worth the same
as yours is not the proper game,
can we, together, act.

So, People, junk the populists (this is a dog's opinion)
and be yourselves, not someone's minion
or happy slave.
Rise up, cast off those 'disillusioned' chains
And 'left behind by globalization' claims;
stand up, take power, don't play their games.
Be brave.

In fact I've just decided that I too
will join your happy fightback crew
this minute!
No leash, no collar, no restraining chain,
no doggie-coats against the rain.
And that long lead (the biggest pain)
I'll bin it.

Freedom at last will come from saying: No!
and liberation's heady wine will flow.
Unleash your power.
This is no time for isolation, hate,
or banning strangers at the gate,
make all of us – together – 'Great'
and seize the hour.

THE MUSEUM OF TRUTH

Ars Poetica

What kind of poems do you like?
The ones that lift the world,
as one might raise a glass,
just polished, to the light
and fiercely search
for any smear or crack.

An Appointment with the Devil

He kept coming round, each time in a new disguise:
those famous horns capped in a daft beanie
on which was embroidered (red on black) *Bad Boy!*

Once, as a carpenter, nicely pleased with himself,
stroking with podgy hands the grain of a new sill;
another time as plumber, hunting a sly leak in the loft.

She stood at the ladder's foot handing up a torch.
Now the dog can see the rabbit! said the voice above the legs
as he scrambled in the rafters quietly cursing.

Once as boiler-man, taking out his big spanner
to twist (*heavy breathing*) a recalcitrant brass nut
and curse again the world of the unyielding.

Then the clumsy proposition at the door
that was quickly closed, her back against it:
her breath coming faster than the slam of a bolt.

The Museum of Truth

They could not tell me where it was
though some had heard its name

so I was left to wander through the streets,
down futile avenues, around locked squares.

I had imagined Doric porticos,
a row of railings capped in gold

but when I found it, on the city's edge,
(in time for 'last admission of the day')

it was a bleak and shuttered barn:
raw concrete streaked by lines of rust.

A bald custodian was at an outside tap,
softening his brittle crust of bread.

He turned with an unpleasant grin
and spat into a nettle-bed.

Inside, the rooms were dusty,
cabinets were draped in sheets,

and on the walls in heavy frames
stiff portraits of the powerful dead.

The prize exhibit was that shining car
they gave the Leader for Inauguration Day.

I imagined shiny tubas, booming drums
beaten by boys in uniform,

high-kicking majorettes
lining that long boulevard

he drove down to the place of power:
the pennants have faded that fluttered then.

He spoke the Truth, they said,
and every word was like a plaque

fixed to a towering wall of fame,
each chiselled letter speaking to the crowds

who later came with tears, and flowers
to heap upon his alabaster monument.

The Lampedusa Cross

Sea-thrown, retrieved
by the island carpenter

who shaped these fragments
of a painted hull

(green-yellow-blue)
into a slender cross

its arms outstretched
to offer comfort

to the wave-washed
driven to the shore

carrying their grief
like a question put

again and again
to the snapping wind.

God

I cannot think now when our dialogue ended,
when we decided to call it a day,
when I slipped my arms in the long sleeves of a winter coat
and, nodding farewell, clicked the door shut.

I cannot say if the wind blew or the rain sheeted,
or whether the sun broke quickly behind a cloud
making the asphalt steam where scattered petal and seed
stuck to the warm surface in pink and white.

I cannot recall either time or season, whether I was young or old,
nor if my mood was truculent or simply perplexed.
I am certain something was left after the long conversation
but the warp and woof of it has slipped my mind.

I cannot say if that is it, if the party is truly over,
if I must really pack for good and take the prints from the wall,
burn redundant letters, scribble out a forwarding address,
or whether . . .

The Dead

This is strange, for I thought that our business was done
when I caught myself climbing up to the porch
where a glossy black car was imperiously parked
and I turned in mid-quip to catch sight of the box
whose varnish and brasses now brought me up short.

I thought you were gone, the tensions and errors
of judgement and speech, that we were both guilty of,
settled and finished, our accounting all done,

all the tackle cleared out from the scatter on deck,
all sorted and shaken and ship-shape and coiled.

This is strange: how you come to remind me of this:
that things are unfinished, that it's madness to think
that nothing at all now remains to be said,
when the opposite palpably beats on the mind
and the heart, and still we must try what we can.

So make the first move, fire the opening gun,
tell me the things that you struggled to say
and intend to resume as we gather our blotters
and fidget our hands on the table's green-leather,
the copier's agenda just falling, clack-clack.

Can we conjure from silence the talk we evaded
and start to sketch out the chat we'd have had?
I'd start but in seconds dry up and then stammer
while you watched with your vigilant, ruminant eye
and out of your silence at last I would get it:

that nothing we say can possibly change
what runs like a river under the stones
where we walk, where silence is natural,
where talking's approximate, and nothing
is something, something to say.

Savages

All praise to Sir Humphrey Gilbert
on his voyage to Newfoundland.
All praise to the canny knight
as he stalked the damp strand

on that June morning by the sea,
kicking the shell and rubbery wrack,
sniffing the clean air
from the hills at his back.

His strategy that day
was neither wavering nor feeble:
Morris dancers, hobby-horses and May-like conceits
to delight the 'savage' people

whom by all fair means possible.
he would win on the fringed beach.
No need of the gallows-tree,
for the lesson he would teach.

No crack and smoke
of musket and powder,
with subtler ways to lay out
the plain text of power.

No doubts of dominion
as they drew from the hold
this cargo of persuasion,
bright reds and greens and gold

to dazzle the silent people,
watchful and awakened.
Who weighed this freight
in a scale of their own making.

Yggdrasil

In Norse mythology the ancient evergreen tree of fate, under which the
gods sit in council and which upholds the universe; a yew, or an ash.
– *A Dictionary of English Plant Names*, Geoffrey Grigson

Grey day in Radnor,
the shaken sheet of rain,
flicked forward by the great ash
that towers above my house

where the nuthatch zigzags
and small twigs, knuckled,
fall to the grass, dry out
and are broken with a snap.

I cannot hear the gods,
murmuring in conference.
They are not quarrelsome Greeks
but Northerners, taciturn,

leaning on the pommels
of their long swords,
moved to speech
slowly, with reluctance,

baffled by the madness
of the occupants
of this world of men
and women

under the dripping ash
with its bark of silver grey
and those tipped buds of black
where the leaf will open.

Old Llywarch

I

I was the ash with its crown of bright leaf
but the weather destroyed it, forced it aslant.
Lightning unmade it, and savage the grief
that came to reward my arrogant youth.

My songs were renowned in the log-lit long halls
before I was stooped, as you see me, and coughing;
my praise had rebounded from high palace walls;
what my spear had achieved was matter for story.

I am old, I am broken. I am hurt by the seasons.
Autumn's ripeness rebukes me, Winter's iciness stings,
Spring is the worst for the bitterest reasons:
for no love now prepares for the fullness of Summer.

II

In the heartland of Wales, my heart is now dying.
I am hobbled and sick and shunned by the living.
See the stag leap! See the horse's mane flying,
as the daredevils gallop, leaping the hedgerows!

Where are the fields where my banner unfurls?
Where are the hills, unveiling at dawn?
Where did they go, the soft-treading girls
who slipped from my bed in a rustle of silk?

No accident this, no random, chance dealing.
Fate planned it, declared it the price of my living.
My body's dissolving; the world is revealing
each day what I'm bound for: the ruin of Llywarch.

III

Old men are despised for their pantomime weakness:
their stumbling antics, mouths ugly and gaping,
self-hating rebuke, remorse, but not meekness,
for arrogance still breaks out in their insults.

Nothing justifies this, let me warn the unready:
the young and the bold for whom age is a fiction.
You think yourselves certain and your progress so steady,
but my fate shall be yours, and your future as hateful.

Flood

Here is a man,
thinking of a woman,
wanting to bridge
the swift-flowing river
that brings whole trees
from a violent flood
in its turbulent water;
the roof of a house;
an abandoned car;
a terrified horse
screaming its pain.
The woman appears
on the far bank,
in a blue dress,
signalling her love
but he cannot hear her words
which the wind steals
so there is nothing left
but her silence
and her blue dress

and her eyes which say
that she would cross the river
if it could calm itself
after the flood;
that they would bridge
the swift-flowing water;
that they would join
like the two segments
of a sliced pear
someone has parted
with a clean knife.

Ballad

As I went out one morning,
when Autumn leaves were dry;
I found it hard to credit
the brilliance of the sky.

I looked into its blueness
and felt the warming sun
then turned towards the city
for my day had just begun.

I saw the slumped night-workers
asleep in crowded trains;
I saw the cocky bankers
as they plotted easy gains.

I saw a silent chippie,
with a toolbox and a saw;
among the posh commuters
his eyes were on the floor.

I read the morning headlines
on someone else's *Mail:*
a TV chef was cheating
and Curry's had a sale;

and in a distant war-zone
a hospital was razed;
I saw the children running
as their houses blazed.

I left at Covent Garden,
the sun was still as bright;
and Europe's offshore island
was tucked up trim and tight.

The Riddle of the Ampersands

Who was that boy I saw you with,
the one with the lime-green hair?
What did it mean, the two of you,
transformed on the quay to a pair?

Your hand & hand, your lips & lips,
your tattooed anchors matching.
It's more than any girl can bear;
an itch she's wildly scratching.

Why did you leave me there, my love,
where the boats come in from the sea?
Why am I mocked with you & him
and the two of you fancy free?

Why do I walk past the yellow nets
with pain & grief in my heart?
Why does the bitter truth declare
that you & I must part?

What did she have, your brand new girl,
apart from her braids of gold?
Couldn't we talk & twine our hands?
Why should love's trust be sold?

The heart has a store of rotten tricks
for a love like yours & mine;
there's nothing built between me & you
that its skill can't undermine.

I thought our love was like the stone
of the glistening harbour wall;
The iron rings that bound us both
could never let us fall.

The lobster pots are lifted now,
the boxes stacked on the quay;
but all I see in that crowded scene
is the shadow of you & me.

I wish you well, because my love
could never intend you harm,
but I wish once more that you & I
could walk here, arm in arm.

THE YELLOW WHEELBARROW

The Yellow Wheelbarrow

(After William Carlos Williams)

so little depends
on what *I*

think
of the

yellow plastic
wheelbarrow

which has
become

a tank
in which

a blanched
earthworm

fails
to swim.

Movement

You pass into another room.
The décor is surprising.

Gone are the cracked plaster,
the broken sash-cord,

the worn carpet and a sofa
whose innards oozed.

Now there are peaches in a glass bowl
on a table-top of veined marble;
a Cornish beach in oils shows an upended
fishing boat, a tump of yellow net.

You unlock yourself.
You let the rush of morning in.

The Tower

I met a poet, pointing a barrow of bricks,
the forewheel ploughing a slope.

Why are you pushing this load? I said.
Then, sensing wordplay was expected:

What is the burden of your burden?
Where does the tendered wheel tend?

I am building a house, he said,
a house of stone that a tower will top.

Up this ramp foundations lie
for I know the first thing about how to build:

I shall make my house on firm ground,
unlike this slip and slush where my wheel sticks

on its journey upwards to the site on the cliff
with a glorious view of the bay in all weathers.

(I thought you would like that brochure-touch,
that cocktails-at-dusk round the blue pool.)

Though in fact I am making a trim tower
facing everywhere and nowhere, light-bright.

I will live there and write on blank pages,
the script will crawl like the quick adder

that slips through the long, dry grass,
with arcane knowledge of its destination.

My plan will be simple: to catch my meaning,
(if you catch my meaning) hoping to surprise.

For this is the chimera I chase, the private prey,
the decisive moment when the words pounce

like the lepidopterist's net on fluttering life
that beats its wings for a long moment

before the net is lifted
and the sky reclaims what it lent briefly.

I could talk for hours to avoid writing;
I prefer to build, hauling my red bricks

up this eternal slope where the mud slides and
in winter snow lingers in the deep ruts . . .

for I am at my best in the light of spring dawn,
the promise of morning a temptation,

when the scratch of my pen
can be heard on dry paper,

as a cloud of starlings noisily swells
above the stilled cypress trees

and somewhere a chapel bell
summons the day to action.

At such times (I like to say) the odour of paradise
seeps slowly into my writing-room . . .

So, when the tower is done and the slates all fixed;
when the glazing glints and the boards gleam,

I'll be ready to start. Or will there always be diversion?
On days when the carpet-fitters come

with their sharp knives and inimitable banter,
bundling fat rolls from their parked vans,

stripping the green polythene with simian grace,
making obvious comments on the view.

Or the building inspector with her hard hat
and yellow waistcoat, flaps her clipboard

as if it were a signal to distant shipping:
come rescue me from the dark brigand on the clifftop.

There will be gatherings on summer days;
poets and artists, careful of their image,

storing like squirrels the matter of memoir,
making notes on the windy terrace where thyme

puffs its tang and bouquet on that famous wind
that rattles the panes at the end of summer.

There will be days and nights after this is done,
after the last barrow of lime or plaster

stutters like speech to a final stop and stalls
and I watch it, upended, waiting to sink

beneath burying weeds, like a fisherman's smack
his heirs won't care for, letting it rot.

So get out of my light, if I may be so brusque.
I am a poet and have my building to accomplish.

Thief

Ther cam a privee theef men clepeth Deeth,
That in this contree al the peple sleeth
– Chaucer, *The Pardoner's Tale*

I caught him in the act,
that sly intruder.

No striped jersey
or sack marked SWAG

but a natty designer suit
of soft Italian silk.

He smiled easily,
confident in his strength.

He knew the ropes;
doors opened at a touch.

He had refined his kit
to a leather pouch

crammed with small tools
that could pick a lock

with the pecking swiftness
of a small-beaked bird:

I have what I want,
I would not even say

that I abuse my power
to lift life like a watch

left carelessly on the side,
gold lid wide open,

a stillness in the room
magnified by its tick.

I hardly blinked
and he was gone.

A Week of Dreams

Monday
She called me to her basement room.
A plate of figs was waiting,
and we talked of our shared love
for the quirky fictions of Georges Perec

until the postman hammered on the door
with a parcel from Guatemala, stamped
exotically and tightly bound with string.
When unwrapped a little book fell free

in which twelve sonnets, each page
bordered by bright blue butterflies,
told a story of love that had failed
because of the indifference of the beloved.

Tuesday
I was running beside a road of furious traffic,
pursued by angry cyclists on the noisy gravel.
They tipped me to the harsh thorns of a wild hedge.
Blood popped on my punctured arms and legs.

My plimsolled feet splashed in pools that stank
of some foul substance that I knew was toxic;
my cinder track stretched up to a horizon
that spoke clearly of imminent storm.

Wednesday
On the lake a single sail, a tilted hull
watched from the tall window.
A swarm of bees hurl themselves against
the pane, dropping one by one

as if the game exhausted them,
as if there were no end in view
except extinction, a manic erasure,
their corpses fallen in an amber drift.

Thursday
Here I am, striding out across the square,
towards a raft of ribboned generals
patiently awaiting the salute,
the tanks drawn up, the band prepared

to lift their trumpets, thwack the drums,
and march towards the empty space
that I have left, insurgent, arms outstretched
towards the rifle's urgent crack.

Friday
Darkness, flame in the dark pines
that run towards the sea;
a racing of wolves, teeth bared,
a savage barking.

That is a scream I hear, *ob scena,*
an absent fear that chills me,
vicarious pain, a twisting in the gut,
a distant crying for release.

Saturday

And everywhere bunting, deceitful,
fluttering in the morning sunlight
to celebrate another arrival
whose welcome is a trap,

its jaws closing on the taken bait
before the frightened eyes know
the trick that's played on them,
the laughter on the podium.

Sunday

I woke to a shaft of bright sunlight,
a sky whose clarity was a rebuke
to the vividness of imagining,
to the indulgent running of fear.

I take a glass of fresh juice,
listen to the kettle's music,
catch in my nostrils
the shock of coffee freshly ground.

A Short History of Ethics

Much has been written
on the subject of The Good.
It echoes like a gong

calling us from our sins.
It could be painted
as a bright sun between fronds

of the thrashing sycamore,
a dish of brilliance,
a bright target.

And all around it
what looks like the halo
plaster saints wore

in the dark churches of my youth:
made of tin, tarnished,
but operative as an example.

The Way

He came off the mountain in the last of the sun,
leaving the coolness of his summer cave;
winter was breaking, frail ice on the tarns.

We mustered to help but his needs appeared few;
his day was complete with stillness or prayer;
we watched as his smile spread like a stain.

All summer we felt his invisible presence
but when he announced his intention to leave
as the first snows whitened the slopes

we privately uttered a sense of relief.
We couldn't quite take the pressure of Good
that left our small vices nowhere to hide.

Museum Piece

Here is God, with his crucified son
clamped tight between his knees;
on Christ's head sits
the dove of the Spirit
at the level of the Father's groin.

In this way the sculptor
bodied forth the Trinity,
which, as a child in a class
of small, scraped chairs,
I struggled to make sense of.

God the Father, God the Son,
and God the Holy Ghost.

I liked the Spirit best,
thinking birds free to pass
silently through the air:
no sound reaching us
from the far-off beat of wings.

Don't

It's a rope bridge
whose planks are swaying

The wind counsels:
don't do it, hold to the solid land.

Get a grip on silence, whatever
you say, say nothing.

But whoever listened to good advice?
So we mount the rocking stairway,

the shaken carpet of weathered slats
that lurch and slap then tumble us

through chill, ungracious air
into the deep ravine.

The Empty Book

*An Empty Book is like an Infant's Soul, in which any thing may be Written.
It is Capable of all Things, but containeth Nothing. I have a Mind to fill this
with Profitable Wonders.*
– Thomas Traherne

It is a white space
where any act of love
may be performed;

whose primped pillows,
and starched sheets,
wait to be disordered.

Here is spoor of print,
marks that tell
of something live

that has crossed the
empty space,
leaving its trace

like the thin coil
of the sand-worm
on a hard beach

as waves recede
disinclined to wipe
the fresh inscription.

Venus

The painting by Lucas Cranach the Elder, 1531

A girl of Saxony, I'd guess,
disposed by Northern weather
to avoid these naked shows,

persuaded by the painter
to undress inside a room
where ice made dragons

on the window-pane
and lust froze up before the twist
of water left the opened tap.

We Must Avoid Cliché

Colleagues, we are ignoring the elephant in the room!
The Head of Marketing is holding her nose,
(painted fingernails a scarlet clamp).
The furrowed hide heaves, ears ripple,
and that wild trunk
sweeps the teacups to the floor.

Your safety is our primary concern.
(and profit, and the pleasure of dominion,
as we watch you crawl along the aisle
whimpering like a beaten dog).

We must reject one-size-fits-all-solutions.
Come to the long room where bald men,
tape measures round their necks like stoles,
dart at your crotch with a knuckle of chalk.

Heart-stopping: brain-stopping.

This long-awaited first collection.
Long-touted on Twitter by its friends,
its enemies not yet found, still to stir
from their long sleep of indifference.

Give us our country back!
It was here a moment ago, I swear.
The empty cupboard had something in it
but I no longer remember what it was.

There is an old Chinese proverb:
May you live in interesting times.
Colleagues, we are living in interesting times.
(That man in the fourth row, his mouth a cavern
open to the salt winds, his eyes closed
in the condition of the fortunate dead.)

Justified Poem

It's how we might like it: the end resembling the beginning
neat at both ends and the starting out ending so handsomely,
trim and solid, a block of raw text that signals its substance
with none of the ragged, unkempt sprawl of the unjustified.
It's how we might like it for ourselves, in life I mean to say,
not quite the same thing as centring a vase or flower tub
but starting well and ending in the same fashion: promise of
symmetry, the dark lift of a monument of tall, black marble
whose carved gilt letters memorialise some ancient heroine
and pronounce, in Augustan periods, the honourable life span
in extravagant terms that a later age finds far too mellifluous:
but in the end it won't work for each life must be all random
and formless, and know each minute on the brink of disorder.

JIGGER

The Last Bus Home

On Stanley Road, the turfed-out drinkers,
all their bevvies ended; white-shirted bellies

puffed sails, billowing at the street's corner.
They are going home – but not just yet.

There's blathering in the night air
outside a dozen corner pubs.

Those white bellies luminous moths
in the dark night of the city.

The Curve

First witness of transgression,
watching the men with sideburns

leap to the rear platform of the bus
in its long curve to the Pier Head,

across the wide piazza: the fine swagger
as they leap off, ticketless, insouciant,

steady on their feet like mariners
holding their balance on a plunging deck.

Zero Hours

A stand of men in belted macs,
flat caps, black boots.
See them as trees, black and green, t
heir mossed trunks glistening.

This man with fingers cut
and bruised from work
probes silently to fix
a broken mower on the lawn;

tells the young boy
what he should know:
 when men leapt on
each other's backs

to catch the foreman's eye,
begging for the *sou* of work.
'Get down, men,' he says.
'Where's yer dignity?'

A cough, a straightened back,
a finger wiped across the nose:
'I'm as 'umble as a beggar
burra've got me dignity.'

Jigger

We ran down the jigger. Past paint-peeled doors
that closed each tiny yard behind the back-to-backs,
we kicked and scarpered, but nothing happened:
no bugger in shirt sleeves came out shouting;
no prune-faced dog offered us its teeth;

no shrill voice screamed; no threats, no chase,
no scuffer bashing his boots on the flags.
What's mischief for, if no one notices?

Later, such light transgressions yielded
to the more painful, practised wrongs

it is our triumph to excel at.

Patina

After the night-storm, out on the river,
we woke to splashes on the window pane,

light spattering of ochre sand
new rain would wipe away.

Down on the lawn, fragments of leaf,
a plant askew, a clay pot upended.

The day shown through a new lens
wiped with a soft, silk cloth.

The Back of My Hand

Look here: the private map
no expert could read better.

The faint white scar
a farm fork gashed

on a midden in South West Lancashire:
first job, first blood.

More jobs to come, shuffling paper
into patterns of absurdity,

wasting the hours, the weeks,
in gainful employment,

pacing dreams against the clock,
the slow sweep of its slender hand.

Smallholding

The city is losing its grip.
The suburbs gather to a question:
can we survive the encounter with cold fields
and their rows of turnip and beet, turned by
the silver blades of a plough, a flutter
of shrieking gulls rising above the earth?

Loose dogs of the savage kind
throw themselves against wire, howling
for our blood as we trespass harmlessly
across derelict land, daring each other on,
or digging for the remnants of old clay pipes
near a sweet shop, tiny and fragile as a shed.

Cinders and amateur landfill,
abandoned junk, a spewing mattress,
corrugated iron and everything malformed
and jagged and unlovely stacks itself
and is wrapped in the tendrils of bindweed,
white trumpets of convolvulus.

A place that through the years has receded,
my grip on it tenuous, memory
working now to retrieve it, a mad machine,
pumping and wheezing, blowing steam;
its clanking parts rattle and shake,
but only straws on an empty belt emerge.

Rooted

It might happen here: on a beach of hard sand
studded with niggardly shells, fringed with wrack:

Memory strains to recapture
its point of departure, the first scurrying steps,

that have ended here, on a winter's morning,
sunlight on the smooth surface, a scatter of tracks

where the seabirds run in eccentric circles,
just able to withstand buffets of wind.

It might happen here that something is grasped
that cannot, at last, be relinquished.

The silent child at the upper window
watching the coasters' ponderous progress

on a grey sea, under a grey sky, frozen
in endless afternoon boredom.

Somewhere a siren cries out
its strident warning to the day.

It might happen here that a deal is done
with greedy creditors; the nib scratches

a compliant signing, a willingness to yield
to the insistence of belonging

to this place. The wind chases light sand
along the flat beach, driftwood lies

at casual angles and the walkers of dogs
strain their eyes to the shore, to the sea.

It might happen. It might happen. Here.

The Boy

Look! Look now
at his blackened feet,
running, running

on the round cobbles
of the long street
that dips to the river,

only to meet
the massive walls
of an unseen dock.

Give that boy shoes,
give him striped socks,
give him leather laces

drawn in a tight bow.

Three Brothers

Christmas morning.
Coming across the lawn,
three short men in Sunday suits.

Try it again
with four sisters:
uncles and aunts,

bearers of gifts
to the children who watch
from an upper window

already tearing the starred
and reindeered paper off.

Here

Here is a man whose mind has gone,
who drops from an upper window
to the soft, accommodating earth.

Here is the squad-car pausing
on the smooth camber of the asphalt road,
lifting him gently in the mild midnight.

Here is the high hospital tower,
its lights all glaring, its moat of cars:
open all hours, a store of convenience.

Here is the white, high-sided cot
where with my mother I contend
to tug the sheet that shields his modesty.

Here is the innocence of a child.
Here is the fierce, bright light in his eye.
Here is my father, dying.

Mnemonic

I lift the brass bell:
a woman in full skirt,
in whose folds
black stain lingers
after my diligent steel wool
has scoured time's tarnish.

Holding her head
between finger and thumb,
letting her swing,
I hear a sweet tinkle
under her skirts,
but who am I calling?

From my mother I accept
this not-quite-heirloom,
for she has moved away
from the burden of things
having no need, in her late days,
for the clutter and echo of stuff.

Afterwards

Afterwards, when he had 'gone'
she walked to where the car was parked.

It was that coat of ice,
glueing the wipers to the screen,

that did it, broke the seal,
and let it out.

Give 'it' what name you like,
the frozen ground

made the tears flow
as in legend from a struck rock.

Wodge

I'd like to think it was our tongues
(recalcitrant, not coldly mocking)
that made the new boy into "Wodge".
The best that we could do.

So Wodzinski, the doctor's son,
shared my double-desk
and when his lid was lifted
the mess was mesmerising.

This was primal chaos:
torn jotters, chocolate wrappers,
broken pencils, various kinds
and orders of abandoned food.

I think of him now as a surgeon,
bow-tied, sleek, a gracious manner
towards the parents of the child
whose tumour he has neatly taken out.

Parbold

In a Lancashire church you left your hat,
its abandonment transformed into a legend.

Why did you not go back? Why did it sit
for ever on a polished bench, unclaimed?

What kind of hat was it? One of your pork-pies
of green tweed with that central crease or fissure?

Or a more stylish trilby, a little forties,
a little noir, like the titfer of a private dick

walking the night in his long coat (to strident music)
while the villain gave it wellie in a finned car?

We will be like you, leaving stories behind,
half-finished, puzzling, with no point.

Proverbs Subverted

Too few cooks spoil the broth:
give me a crowd, stomachs pressed against the copper,
stirring vigorously with their great wooden spoons.

Two birds in the hand are worth one in the bush.
Trussed for the oven, their plump sizzle and crackle
drowning the sound of that solitary chirp in the myrtle hedge.

Rarely a slip between cup and lip:
the first instinct right and true,
the brimful glass lifted smartly and swallowed.

Don't look before you leap
lest the view from the tor, dizzying and steep,
crumples resolve, liberates a thousand doubts.

Better never than late: the moment lost,
the word stillborn, the smile dying
when once it lived.

Beggars are choosers; their freedoms flower
in a space of their own making: unsalaried,
untenured, free as the loping, long-eared hare.

Bite the hand that feeds you: relish the sharp *Miaou!*
of the fatcat, nursing his bleeding paw.
That will teach the bastard!

There's no time like the past,
before the wobbling wheel met the precipice,
before a cry ricocheted from the loose scree.

A Premature Request

Without wishing to be prescriptive
in the matter of main course or starter
please put out a plate
of my favourite black olives of Kalamata.

As for what not to do: black ties, long faces,
the obvious signs of grieving
– you should think of it as a party
after someone's leaving.

Keep speeches short and the wine flowing,
for an empty glass is a vile offence
and what is a party but corks popping
and everything in the present tense.

CITY LIGHTS

City Lights

1

The city's lights are torches
flickering on a lawn

It will be humid when we land:
the cafés not yet shut

moth-white djellabas
flitting on the street

and a man on a bicycle
pedalling slowly

into a pool of light
where a fluttering palm

dances to the wind's tune
its head tossed back

careless of what might follow
in the slow light of dawn.

2

The privilege of flight:
to look, like Gods, on the small

doings of humankind
along their streets at night

where lamp-standards stretch
their caring arms and weep

small sprinklings of light
over the dusty streets

and two women breathe
the hookah's sweet smoke

at a round table by the kerb
lit by a neon's angry glare.

3

From the long bay we turn
towards the warning flashes

that edge the tarmac strip
to keep us into line:

grounded Olympians,
we come to terms with Earth.

In the vast hall of tumbled baggage
we pull the fragments of our lives

into a seeming shape,
present our papers

to the men in crumpled uniform
whose coldness seems to say:

*your life is nothing, you have come
from nowhere, and soon must leave.*

The Inkwell

. . . even though nothing truly merits the love of any soul, if, out of sentiment,
we must give it, I might just as well lavish it on the smallness of an inkwell
as on the grand indifference of the stars.
– Fernando Pessoa, *The Book of Disquiet*

Sunk in its socket on the grubby desk
the inkwell with its egg-white gloss
in our Sixties classroom (already obsolete).

I am worshipper of small things:
le petit bonheur, a fallen apple moist in grass,
its skin unblemished by the drop;

sepia spots on the endpaper of a favourite book;
the angle of your black beret as I straighten it
like a parent, anxious at the school gates.

The Snatchback Man

His job to knock on doors,
unsavoury canvasser
not foiled by twitched curtain
or slammed back gate.

Aitch-pee, the never-never,
means it's never yours,
loaned like a library book
at the disposal of the law,

which states that time's long reach
can lift a telly from its stand
and put it in a small squat van
leaving you quietly stuffed.

We pay for our illusions
which were not illusions
but meant to be a canny sense
of what might work

(and often does) until the habit
turns into a cocky swagger –
until possession's shown
no fraction of the sodding law.

In my father's school
the newest teacher,
slightly jack-the-lad,
in drainpipe trousers

sideburns slick as Elvis,
a white Cortina parked outside,
joked of his dangerous past
as nifty snatchback man.

Betws-y-Coed

Vandals to the Welsh language, we called it 'Betsy Co-ed'
What do you expect from two teenaged, pimply, Scouse,
shambolic campers, tyro boozers, adepts of minor mayhem,
(though well-behaved inside the snug of the blue slate hotel)?

As the night wore on and the glasses, like the towers of a town,
crowded to the slopped table's brass-bound rim,
the language sang around us like a chamber piece:
'It's all right, lads, (near chucking-out) *we're not talkin' about you!'*

The Six-Shooter

The squeak of rubber wellingtons
tramping the stone slabs of a narrow alley;
a silver pistol in its holster, primed with caps,
a cowboy hat with tasselled fringe, a Sheriff's star.

'Mongol' the term we used in those rough days.
'Down's Syndrome' now – more kindly done.
At this same alley's mouth one boy pointed to the sky:
That's called a formation. Words were beginning

a long enchantment, always ready to surprise:
epistemology, supererogatory, disestablishment.
At the same time the lure of the fierce and plain,
like the terms of love or *Bang! Bang! You're dead!*

The Song of Rhodri

Rhodri Goch, an imaginary medieval bard living in the Welsh Marches

I have placed my hut
under the stolid oak

near the sharp thorns
stark in winter;

the holly too
with its red berries

can scratch my flesh:
so many sharps!

  ★

The oak's immensity,
ungraspable girth,
makes me slap its flank;
a big man at a big tree

I am gifted with movement,
no tunnelling root
holds me down
as I move through meadows.

*

Winter is my season:
the drifts of pure snow

under the blackthorn,
unbudded hazel,

ice on the still pond
and a keen wind

blowing through Radnor,
a hook's swift slice.

*

I doubt the summer:
its soft airs

and sweet flowers,
the squeak of grass

in the mouth of ewes,
soften resolve.

I am happy
in harsh weather,

my face wet
with melting hail.

*

The harpist comes;
her rapid fingers

pick and pluck;
I beat the stretched tabor.

From the wood's heart
they come in ones and twos

to hear her play
a drawing music.

She sings, the birds
an unsought choir;

she sings to me
in my cold season

where the shattered snail
that the blackbird batters

on his anvil stone
leaves brittle fragments.

*

O Rhodri Goch,
your vivid hair

autumnal apple leaf
before frost furs the bark.

Big-boned and broad
as your companion oak

you swing your axe,
making short work of it.

At your hut's threshold
the fire lingers;

acorns underfoot
crackle and split.

In the thick woods
they are trimming bows,

stringing for war
along the March.

     *

Whether the king sleeps
until the hurt land

wakes him to redemption
I cannot say, but the tales

are all around me
in her songs launched

in the wet forest
under canopies of leaf.

     *

O Rhodri Goch,
tall man of the green woods

where the brook races
over the black stones,

down to the valley
where mist lingers

and the hare lifts its ears,
suspecting danger.

The Disappeared

Well-mannered, taking their time,
they watch us from the wings.
No rush to judgement,
rather a ruminant silence:
slow beasts shut in a long shed,
chewing their bales of shaken hay.

They were present once
with sharp tongues,
long ripples of companionable laughter,
flashing zig-zags of wit.
But now their talk is gone;
they are watchers and waiters.

Sometimes a sound betrays them,
an ugly clatter, a distant slam,
the scatter of broken glass.
Then the night is still again:
wine revolved in a glass,
held to the light for its ruby glow.

The Dark

Come down into the dark:
the lights are off,
a milky moonlit rope
partners the twisting stair.

I like the gloom;
so spare of light.
It is a board
on which a stick of chalk

draws vivid figures:
a goat with butting horns,
a sleekly sinuous snake,
some people by a lake

whispering softly
in a puzzling language,
their fur hoods
hiding their hair

but not the eyes
which glitter
as points of fire
in a night-time landscape.

Come down into the dark
where anything may happen;
where dreams collide
like knocking boats.

In Praise of the Washington Metro

At Metro Center we're industrious as elves
busy in high-vaulted caves; the cars glide in
and everyone rushes when the music stops

to find a seat and stay right in there, in the game.
This way and that – up here, down there –
we're rushing, they're rushing, to get ahead.

O Foggy Bottom, Shady Grove, who christened you?
The tunnellers beneath a wooded, swampy place
where once the originals galloped and cried?

Or clever makers of new maps, new names,
dipping cupped hands in Silver Spring,
smiling on our stop, called Friendship Heights?

Europe

I call you a lake
on which our boat
(red-white-and-blue)
glides under sail.

The island nation
whose anchor rattles
down-down-down
to a bed of sand.

The same wave
slaps our hull;
the same wind
flaps the jib.

The lake has room
for numerous craft.
Windermere-wide,
it feels fathomless.

We have our quirks,
our captain's jokes.
You mend your nets,
squatting like a tailor

in an old print.
From a quayside cafe
there is laughter
and the chink of glasses.

There is room for all
on the lake's surface;
the far hills at sunset
are bathed in light.

Were it not for the flags
we should not know
one from the other
as the boats skip by.

Ballad

As I went out one morning,
when Autumn leaves were dry;
I found it hard to credit
the brilliance of the sky.

I looked into its blueness
and felt the warming sun
then turned towards the city
for my day had just begun.

I saw the slumped night-workers
asleep in crowded trains;
I saw the cocky bankers
as they plotted easy gains.

I saw a silent chippie,
with a toolbox and a saw;
among the posh commuters
his eyes were on the floor.

I read the morning headlines
on someone else's *Mail:*
a TV chef was cheating
and Curry's had a sale;

and in a distant war-zone
a hospital was razed;
I saw the children running,
their neighbourhood ablaze.

I left at Covent Garden,
the sun was still as bright;
and Europe's offshore island
was tucked up good and tight.

Love in Six Bullet Points

• One may kiss in many places
  but the lobe
  is a letter away from love.

• The key in the lock
  unlocks the heart:
  you are back.

• In the next room
  I hear a pencil drop;
  my senses sharpen.

• In the heart of the night
  the heat of the night
  is suddenly turned up.

• It was a speck of black
  in a far-off crowd.
  Then it was you.

• I feel the cold fingers
  of those small gloves
  left behind on a chair.

From the Boutique Hotel

Your room is ready and the sheet's turned down
(the pillow dimpled by a star-shaped chocolate).

Steam lingers on the thermal pool
from which you scamper to the towel's warmth.

The manager is young (but has no hair).
His boots a lumberjack's with laces loose.

His desk's a sheet of glass on which a laptop sits;
the T-shirt begs: PLEASE TELL ME YOUR DESIRES.

Along the corridors the women push slow carts,
pausing at certain doors as if they came to pluck

plague-victims for the lime-pit's endless sleep;
silently they disappear through unmarked doors

to bleak, cold rooms where sheets are stacked,
with mops and liquids, where walls are bare.

Everything is sweetness at the Boutique Hotel;
no raucous shouts, no rough and ragged edge.

If we can make your stay more pleasant
nothing would please us more: enjoy!

See how all smile at breakfast, sharing their delight,
as fresh fruit's spooned into a small, cupped bowl;

the yoghurt's surface broken by the first dipped spoon,
(small footprints on a slope of newly fallen snow).

A basket of warm eggs, six kinds of breakfast roll,
a pan of bacon and the glow where toast grows dark.

All this is good, and we feel good just being here,
sweetly embraced by the Boutique Hotel.

Just over there a breakfast meeting's under way,
six people stroking mobiles as they talk.

I do not want to leave this tranquil place
for there is wind outside, a threat of rain.

The staff are kind, the masseuse moves with skilful hands.
There is only kindness here and everything is fine.

The world should be like this, all roughness smoothed.
Surely our wish for it could make it so

Countryman

The saw is on again;
I hear its whine
beyond the trees.

He's lifted off
the jam jar cowl
that tops the pipe

and kicked the engine
into puttering life.
He feeds the teeth

with rough-cut timber,
sliced with a scream
into short lengths

that we will watch
like movie-goers,
as they flame and spit

behind the stove-door glass,
in the surprising cold
of blackthorn weather.

The World Tree

The world tree in Norse mythology, the evergreen ash or Yggdrasil, stands in the middle of the world above the well of fate; its branches extend over all the nine realms. Each realm hangs on its own branch, but if the tree should shake or fall, so will all the realms. The tree has three roots which reach down to the underworld.

Ask

Two wind-dried logs
set in sand-drift on the shore:

the first man and woman,
in the Northmen's story.

The ash tree, Ask, strong hub
on which the globe turns,

its high leaves rustling in the wind,
made the first couple.

This is how stories start,
in a breezy somewhere,

out of chaos, a new line
drawn with a wet nib.

The Nine Realms

Tree of the world, ash canopy,
each realm hangs, dry keys
from a bony-fingered branch

Shake that tree; unsettle it
and the nine realms fall,
ground to destruction.

As the red machine
spits from its spout
a pyramid of chewed twig.

Dieback

The myths recount serpents
with a taste for destruction,
able to gnaw the deep root.

Imperium crumbles:
the medalled autocrat
losing his power

as the tanks draw up
in the palace yard
and rifles snap.

He dips his head
to enter a car
he has not ordered:

moving off too fast
(a bullet through the head
of his usual driver)

he is taken to a room
where there will be
much awkward civility

and a slow disrobing;
the sword in its scabbard
gently prised from his hands.

Tree Surgeons

Swift as monkeys, they swing into the tree,
bounce out on flipped ropes, kick free,

in scarlet helmets knowing no fear,
proud of their tackle and gear.

They disparage the ash,
the tree doomed to crash

and be sliced for the fire.

Leaf

A dry curl falls on the page
before a gust carries it.

Siegfried made vulnerable
where his bath of dragon's blood

– that armour-dye –
left a leaf-shaped space

for Hagen's spear to pierce:
as we always miss

the one raw place
that lets the poison in.

Healing

The axe falls; the white flesh splits;
the blade wedged in its parted "V".

Then the child, weak of breath,
(as once I was on a windy foreshore)

drawn through the healing gap
before they bind again the tree's divided limb.

I drew the cold salt air into my chest,
held my small lapels tight around the neck.

Menagerie

Late winter afternoon and the light failing
but noise still in the limbs' bareness;
a nuthatch hammering, small songbirds trilling,
and a squirrel leaping from branch to branch.

Unseen, the beetle and bug, earwig and borer
in quiet industry chewing and nibbling.
In this way the host, Yggdrasil, let four stags crop
such foliage as they wished, the eagle roost,

mulling its *knowledge of many things,* the squirrel,
Ratatosk (Drill-Tooth) run up the bark
with fresh deliveries of slander, the roots
feel the serpent's destructive fang.

Stoic, as the dark drapes it, patient boughs
waving their frigid welcome to all comers,
settling in for a long night, as the owl
starts to hoot in the near distance.

Woodwork

Out of our wood,
the felled log
taken and trimmed;

kiln-dried and planed,
its pale timber
shaped into this:

a hard bench
whose cross-grained joints,
dark squares of strength,

hold the worked thing
in one piece sawn
and smoothed;

oiled to a shine
that the first beam of morning
rubs like a genie's lamp.

The Poetry Business

Scop, skald or *makar*: call us what you will.
We'll sing for anything you'll throw:
bent bottle-tops, small coins, cheap wine,
or that most frequent dole, a cap of wind.

This craft is never traded on a shouting floor;
we don't wax fat or drive low cars.
If we are spotted with a menu card
it isn't verse that's paid the bill.

GREEK LETTERS

A sequence for the Greek Bicentennial, 2021

Athens

for Alexandros Kypriotis

Another year, Aléxandros, pandemic-penned.
Skipping like mountain goats into the scrub,
we shun, through 'social distance', every friend
whose presence once, in café, bar or pub

perked up our days – to hunch at screens that zoom
when we would speak, desperate to underline
each 'intervention' from our locked-down room:
this clipped *mikrócosmos* where we're confined.

Under that quiet taverna's mulberry tree
in an Athens quarter far from tourist crowds,
where milky ouzo glasses clinked, we three
enacted friendship as the sun went down.

How long before another glass (or two)
is pledged in heartfelt, plain *yiasou!*

Inheritance

We are all Greeks – Shelley

Boat-builders in a dusty yard – their skeleton upraised
above its narrow keel – follow an ancient guide
or template, knowing what works, the trail blazed
by craftsman after craftsman, each cut piece tried

by knowing hands that lift a plank to the light,
shaping, smoothing, testing its strength:
judging what cuts the wave when the wind is right,
grace and energy along its clinkered length.

So thought's first plan, myth's first making,
came from these islands and the baking plains;
found their first trials in a culture waking
out of darkness into its growing pains.

Africa too, the East, built mind-peaks of power;
but from this soil there grew the West's first flower.

Ioannina

The wind-whipped lake ripples and the town
makes preparations for a lively night.
Our small boat from the lake island puts down
its gangplank in the day's dissolving light.

Hatzis, your *End of Our Small Town* makes us believe
we know its story: for those tanners at the castle wall,
practising a dying trade, you do not idly grieve
but show how everything is flux, that empires fall

on truths like this: that nothing lasts, that pride
of citizen or nation must work with process,
with the aching knowledge that we ride
a beast we can't restrain, for history is progress.

The *Agamemnon* tells us *man must suffer to be wise:*
better that brutal truth than self-deceiving lies.

1821

Who fired the first shot? Raised the rebel flag?
Bouboulina, gilded pistol in her belt,
whom no patriarch would dare to gag,
heroine of coin and banknote, icon of revolt?

It must have seemed that all Pandora's box
(as Hesiod describes) of strife and pain
had been uncrated at the Spetsai docks
as violence, killing, vengeance came

to christen the new state with blood
as if the gods required of Greece,
if they would see new freedoms bud
and blossom, a penalty for wanting peace.

The new Republic paid that tax on liberty
in civil war's unchecked ferocity.

Diaspora

Olives of Kalamata swim in plastic bowls.
brine-floated *féta*, elephantine beans,
and that strong smell the exile knows,
excite a longing for abandoned scenes.

In Alexandria, Melbourne or New York
music in cellars concentrates desire;
the tongue of Greece that loves to talk
breaks out like an ungoverned fire.

In the Athenian Grocery, Moscow Road,
packets of *ánithos, paximádi,* capers,
tomatoes waiting for their *yemistá,* are sold
with pastries, *loukániko,* the latest papers.

Elláda has its flags of blue and white.
And scattered music in a foreign night.

Skiathos

I step inside the Papadiamantis house:
the room he slept in like a prison cell,
conceiving there his *Murderess*
whose tale is like a steady chapel bell

that rings out loud and clear above the town
on an island morning from a blue-capped tower
making a music that consorts with stone,
dry gulleys, beating sun, the tiny flower

of thyme and oregano clinging to life
on these harsh slopes where Frankojannou ran,
fleeing, as if pursued by bees, the strife
that stung her woman's life's harsh span.

Admiring tourists on a stubborn rock look down
towards the bay in which her tortured body drowned.

Byzantine

I lift the tiny chapel's latch, tug at the green door,
step in to coolness, incense-trace and bottled oil
for fuelling lamps; a shaft of sun sweeping the floor,
gilding *iconostásis* and the *ex votos'* beaten foil.

I've known, in larger spaces, chants, the smoking thurifer;
received a smile, beneath his tall, cylindrical hat,
from a monk who gave me, as a gift to purify
my stained soul, a wad daubed in holy oil, a cat

raised in his arms as he bade farewell.
Mystrás, the Metéora, strike a grander note
than this: no bigger than a hermit's cell,
but Greece is here, I think, on a remote

hot hillside where the centuries strain
to halt the mind's erasure. They live again.

Kalavryta

In the *kafeneío* old men grip their sticks,
small cups of coffee cluster on the table.
Enter a pedlar with his shepherd's crooks:
a vision lifted from some pastoral fable.

Pretending to ignore the senate's murmurs,
and playing hard to get, he looks away;
experienced fingers feel for firmness,
but make no bids for they have had their day.

Above the town the massacre's monument,
for every victim a small lamp that glows.
But why was this inhuman slaughter sent?
Is there some lesson that this suffering shows?

A sudden breeze blows through the town;
white almond blossom snows the ground.

Freedom

To see the large thing in the small:
a gravestone's blurred Islamic script,
a city re-imagined from a ruined wall,
Venetian castellations time has stripped

of their magnificence become a palimpsest
laid on Hellenic text that says, *we're free.*
The jasmine flower Seferis dressed
as white's eternal brilliancy.

The spirit of a people cannot be concealed
behind an emperor's brocaded robe;
the moth destroys its bright heraldic field
and power crumbles like a shattered globe.

But it's not flags, nor marching bands,
but self-belief by which a nation stands.

Arcadia

A goatherd boy steps out from a concealing bush
tendering a bunch of mountain tea, a faltering smile
blends welcome with a shy retreat; behind him lush
sweet grass of spring, dotted with orchids, while

his goats with clattering bells look on from rocks,
Arcadian rocks of poet's pastoral, the Golden Age
restaged for us: bell, crook, and scattering flocks,
alive, not what you'd see on Loeb's footnoted page.

Cold Northerners, we burn our skin bright red,
seek out the beaches, walks and must-see sites.
The Greece that's here and now, not dead,
contends with the imagined past, new sights

displace the old – until a goatherd on a hill
recalls Theocritus, a world that could be living still.

Notes

Page 45, 'Orpheus'. Lines by Jean Cocteau, painted on his mural at the Salle des Mariages, Hôtel de Ville, Menton. A translation: 'Orpheus, in turning his head, lost his lover and his music. Men became beasts, and the animals savages.'

Page 45, 'Topping Out'. Epigraph translated from *Venises*, by Paul Morand.

Page 79, 'Walk'. Gérard de Nerval made these remarks as he walked his pet lobster, Thibault, on its lead in the grounds of the Palais-Royal. His friend Théophile Gautier recorded them in his *Portraits et Souvenirs Littéraires*. A translation: 'In what way is a lobster any more ridiculous than a dog, a cat, a gazelle, a lion or any other animal that one might take for a walk? I am very fond of lobsters. They are calm, serious, know the secrets of the sea, and they don't bark . . .'

Page 80, 'Annotations of Byzantium'. The principal source of this poem is *The Secret History* by Procopius (translated, as a Penguin Classic, by G. A. Williamson, 1966). Written around AD 550, it is a remarkably candid account of the reign of the Byzantine Emperor Justinian and his wife Empress Theodora, who is the narrative voice in the poem. The most famous of the Byzantine emperors, Justinian assumed power in 518 and married Theodora in 523. She died in 547 and Justinian in 565. Justinian is seen as a great law-giver and the period of his reign saw the construction of the basilica of Agia Sophia ('Holy Wisdom') completed in 537 but Procopius tells a story of vicious corruption and tyranny, greed and lust behind the scenes. He also recounts the story of the general Belisarius, whose secretary Procopius had been, and of his wife Antonina, who it appears was as corrupt as Theodora herself.

Page 111, 'The Lampedusa Cross'. This 40cm high cross was made from fragments of a boat wrecked on 3rd October 2013. The boat was carrying more than 500 refugees and migrants across the

Mediterranean from Africa to Europe. The cross was made by Francesco Tuccio, a carpenter on the island of Lampedusa, as a memorial to the 361 men, women and children who perished in the wreck. It is now on public display in the British Museum.

Page 116. 'Old Lywarch' was suggested by a translation into English prose of the Welsh poem, 'Llywarch Hen' in *A Celtic Miscellany*, edited by Kenneth Jackson and published by Penguin Books.

Page 117. 'Flood' was partly inspired after seeing Theo Angelopoulos's film about refugees, *The Suspended Step of the Stork*, in which a sequence shows the wedding of a young couple while they remain separated by a river marking the border between Greece and Albania.

Page 136. 'Jigger' is the Liverpool word for an entry or alley between back-to-back houses. A 'scuffer' is a policeman.